Live Your BEST Life:

Stories of Triumph

Foreword
by Dr. Ruben West

This joint book features individuals who have faced challenges in their lives but have refused to give up. I have worked with each of these individuals personally and have been amazed as well as inspired by their commitment to overcome their setbacks. Often times, we wonder why life treats us the way it does. If you're anything like me you have faced unforeseen issues, circumstances, and encounters. One of my coaching clients had everything going along just fine and then ran into a financial issue that he never saw coming. This is becoming more and more common because of the challenges in the job market. Technology is rapidly eliminating jobs. It wasn't that long ago that if you wanted to make a long-distance phone call you would call a long-distance operator. Furthermore just a short time ago, if you wanted to go on a vacation or take a trip, you called a travel agent. In both of these instances technology has eliminated the need for these positions and individuals have lost their jobs which caused financial hardships. We will see this more and more often in the near future.

There are many individuals who are struggling in their relationships. This is due in part because of all of the new challenges and demands that life is putting on couples in relationships. People are being asked to do more with less. Parents are doing all that they can to raise their children properly. However with new technology, such as cell phones and internet, children have access to all sorts of information at the click of the button and much of the information is not positive. These issues are increasing the complexity of what was once a simple life.

For these reasons as well as many more it is likely that we will all face setbacks. As a matter of fact I can tell you from my own personal experiences that there are three primary types of problems in life; the ones you've been through, the ones you're going through, and the ones that are waiting for you!

It is with this in mind that we all must have strategies for overcoming setbacks. I believe that sometimes God gives us the advantage of disadvantage. Think about it this way, how many great inventions have we created because of being temporarily disadvantaged? How many times have personal challenges caused an individual to rise up and achieve great success? Has there ever been a heavyweight boxing champion of the world who was born with a silver spoon in his mouth? I think not! It was because of the environment that they were born into, the feeling of being disadvantaged, and the lack of opportunity that drove the beginning boxer to work harder than most people can possibly imagine and push himself to the top of the sport.

Such was the plight of the individuals who contributed to this book. They have all faced challenges and been knocked down by life. But in the words of Mohammed Ali, "The canvas is no place for a champion"! These individuals understood the importance of getting back up on their feet. It wasn't enough for them to just survive, they wanted to thrive. They are not settling for the good life, they were determined to live their best life.

As you read this book you will recognize that all of us have an inner strength that can't be denied. It would be great if we could have our life's path laid out in an easy-to-follow obstruction free roadmap. However, we all know that an easy life does not build strong character. That's why, just when everything appears to be going great, life happens. You get hit with the punch that you didn't see coming. In those times, life is testing you. It's all a part of the character building process. There will be days, weeks, and months in your life where the sun will not light your path. In these circumstances you will have to let your inner light shine. Sometimes you will go the way of the light. Other times, you will have to light the way for others. Either way, commit to doing as these individuals have done. Commit to living your BEST life.

Dedication

At the end of his life George Bernard Shaw was asked this question; "If you had the opportunity to come back and be anybody throughout the course of history, who would you like to come back as?" His answer; "I'd like to be the man I never was."

This book is dedicated to Edwina Blackman. I met Edwina when I was working at a hospital in Wichita Kansas. I remember her saying to me, "Ruben, you can help people, they will listen to you." When she first said these things, they were too hard for me to believe. Fortunately, she was persistent and continued to encourage me every time she saw me. She helped me to become the person that was hidden within me all along.

This book is a representation of the man she helped me become. I have personally worked with each individual in this book helping them to see something in themselves that they didn't see; just as Edwina did for me.

Edwina, thank you for your encouraging words and continual support. You were right, they did listen. My mentor Les Brown says; "Sometimes you have to believe in someone else's belief in you, until your belief kicks in."

I believe.

Ruben West

Table of Contents

Foreword...2

Dedication 6

Copyright Page 8

"THE PUNCH YOU DON'T SEE COMING"...............10

   Roland Manny 10

CREATING A QUANTUM SHIFT.................................38

Carlenia Springer..38

I AM A TESTIMONY...62

   John McClung Jr..62

COMFORTABLE...ARE YOU By Justin G. LaRocque
....80

YOU HAVE EVERYTHING YOU NEED.......................98

   Kimberly Schimmel..98

MORE OUT OF LIFE...118

   DeMetra Moore..118

FEAR CAN DESTROY YOU 134

   Dorian A. Branch Sr. 134

ONE IN A MILLION..144

   By Josh Rios 144

I AM ENOUGH...AND SO ARE YOU!.......................156

   Traci Ward..156

LIFE IS A FIGHT...176

Robin Shyrell...176

Dr. Ruben West...195

Self Published Authors Network

1369 N. HAMPTON RD STE 60

DESOTO TEXAS 75115

ASKJMACK2@GMAIL.COM

WWW.SELFPUBLISHEDAUTHORSNETWORK.COM

Ordering information

Quantity Sales. Special discounts are available in quantity

purchases by corporations, associations, networking groups. For details contact www.SelfPublishedAuthorsNetwork the address above

Individual Sales- Contact Traci Ward

      www.lamenoughtw.com

      Traci.ward40@gmail.com

      785-554-1841

Includes biographical references and index

ISBN-13: 978-0692548691 (Self Published Authors Network)

ISBN-10: 0692548696

"THE PUNCH YOU DON'T SEE COMING"

Roland Manny

Bio

The passion that Roland has for health, nutrition and motivating people led him to **Herbalife International** where he and his team have daily improved the lives of others for over 20 years.

Roland's drive and passion for helping others extends to his public speaking engagements where he is coached and mentored by Dr. Ruben West of the Black Belt Speakers; he is also a Platinum Speaker under the direction of Mr. Les Brown.

Roland is father to Torie and grandfather to Savannah. Roland married his wife Julie in February 2013; they now reside in Dublin, Ohio.

Roland's goal is to help others realize their dreams ARE POSSIBLE -no matter the circumstances.

Sometimes in life when we think everything is going great, when things are going our way, when things could not be any better, we are going to take a "HIT"; and we will never see it coming. It was Muhammed Ali who said "It's the punch you don't see coming that knocks you out." As you are reading this, you may have already been hit, you are getting hit or if not - hold on because it's coming as nobody gets through life without being hit.

For me, the punch I didn't see coming was on September 21, 2009. I can remember it like it was yesterday. I was at Gillette Stadium, home of the New England Patriots. It was a perfect day. The weather was perfect, our seats were perfect, and the atmosphere was perfect. The only thing that wasn't perfect was the fact that the Patriots were getting beat badly by the Miami Dolphins. I remember saying to my friend Jim, "It doesn't get any better than this."

Then, at some point during the game I received a text message and before I responded to the text message I knew something wasn't right. I want you to take a look at your life and see if there was ever a time when you received a text message, or an email, or a phone call, or a knock on the door and before you read the text, or opened the email, or answered the phone, or opened the door you knew something wasn't right. That text I received came from my 15-year-old daughter Torie. My 15-year-old daughter Torie who was brought up in a good Christian family .My 15-year-old daughter Torie who was taught to follow her own morals and values and not to follow the wrong crowd. My 15-year-old daughter Torie who was so gifted in basketball that between her freshman and sophomore years of high school had already drawn the attention of college basketball scouts.

The message read, Hey dad and I knew something wasn't right. I text her back, what's up Tor? The text read dad, I'm pregnant, I'm pregnant; it was the punch I never saw coming. I never expected to see my 15-year-old daughter who hadn't even begun to live life yet pregnant. Sometimes you are going to get hit with the unexpected surprises that life throws at you. Maybe it wasn't that but maybe it was like my brother who had worked for a major corporation for 13 years. Who for 13 years spent weeks at a time away from his family? Who worked 60 to 70 hours a week taking the company from struggling to thriving. Who was always very stressed, worrying if his work was good enough. One day, I received a call from him and he shared with me that he lost his job. When I ask him what happened he explained the new president called him up to her office for what he thought was going to be a routine meeting. When he got to her office she told him the company was moving in a different direction and some changes were being made and that he was no longer needed. She gave him his pink slip. I asked "how long it took her to fire you?" He said it took about 12 seconds. I said will you look at that, your life isn't worth a second a year to them." He got hit by the punch he didn't see coming that was thrown at him by the opponent, Corporate America.

Maybe it wasn't your job, maybe it was the like friend Jeff who received a phone call at 2:00 in the morning from the last person you ever to want to receive a call from at 2:00 am, the local police department. When Jeff answered the phone the officer informed them that they had his son. Jeff said you have the wrong number, my son is in bed sleeping. The officer again said, sir, "we have your son" to which Jeff again said, "My son is in bed sleeping." After being told the third time they had his son, just to prove them wrong , Jeff ran up the stairs, opened the door to his sons' room, turned on the light and when he looked at his sons' bed, he wasn't there.

Jeff ran back down the stairs picked up the phone and said, officer, he is not in his bed to which the officer replied, "That is what I have been trying to tell you. When you were sleeping your son stole your car and we found him on the side of the road. He overdosed on heroin and we had to resuscitate him twice; your son died twice." His 15-year-old son Zack who was brought up in a great Christian family, who was in the top 1% soccer players in the country for his age group, a heroin addict. It was the punch Jeff and Diane never saw coming thrown by the opponent, drug addiction.

Maybe it was like my wife Julie who had a physical and thought that she was in perfect shape. A few months after her physical she started experiencing some issues that didn't seem quite right so she went to the Dr. for what she thought would be a routine exam. A few days after the appointment she received a phone call from her doctor who said the three words nobody ever wants to hear, "you have cancer." Julie, a healthy 46-year-old woman. Julie, a successful business woman with everything going for her. Cancer. It was the punch she never saw coming, thrown by the opponent, the illnesses of life.

I want you to think of a friend or family member who may have been hit with a punch they didn't see coming thrown by the opponent, corporate America, the addictions of life or the illnesses of life.

There I was in Gillette Stadium, 50,000 screaming fans yet I felt like I was all alone. I could have heard a pin drop. I remember looking straight up at the sky like I was flat on my back laying on the canvas of life thinking to myself, her life is ruined, the baby is going to have a tough life, what are people are going to think of me, how am I going to pay for this, a million thoughts running through my head.

Here is what I know, life is like a boxing match. The same characters that are in a boxing match are those same characters in your life. First, there is the opponent that could be the surprises of life, corporate America, drug addiction the illnesses of life. These influences are trying to knock you out and waiting for you to get up only to knock you out again. Then there is the referee, standing over you waiting to count you out but most people do what I did and count themselves out! I did this when I was saying her life is ruined, the baby is going to have a tough life, what are people are going to think of me, and how I am going to pay for this. What most of us do is count ourselves out by saying we aren't good enough, we aren't smart enough, we don't have the education, we don't have the money, we don't the skills, talents or abilities; we count ourselves out.

Then, we can't forget the people in the stands, they are there to see a fight, to see someone get knocked out and they don't even care if it's the champion. Like in a boxing match, in life, people want to see others get knocked out. The people in the stands are there to see someone get knocked out - most of the time these are your friends, your family, your co-workers, your acquaintances, people that you thought you could count on when you got knocked down. What they are really there for is to witness you get knocked out!

To me, the most important person in that ring, in the arena, is that manager, the trainer, the person in the corner because when a boxer is training for a fight, he looks for a great trainer. The trainer doesn't say you're not good enough, you're not fast enough, you don't have the talent, skills or abilities to beat this guy, he's too fast, you lost before, others have lost to him, and you'll never win. NO, he looks for someone who tells him, he can win, he does have the skills, he does have the abilities, he does have the talent, he's has the speed, the where-with-all to go the distance, to win the fight and the heart to do it.

The person in my corner, the person that needed me, the person that was counting on me, the person that was telling me to get off the canvas, the person that needed me to win was my daughter, Torie, shouting get up dad, get up, I need you! I don't just need you when things are good, I need you when things are tough, I need you NOW! You said you would always be there for me. I had to make the decision to do this, I had the make the decision to get up from the canvas and fight for my daughter or be a chump and stay knocked down. I chose to fight, I was her champion.

My question to you is this, when life knocks you down, when you are flat on your back on the canvas of life ready to count yourself out what friend, what family member, what client, what person you haven't even met yet is standing in your corner reaching for you saying, get up, don't quit we need you, we are counting on you, you said you would be there for us and if you don't get up and keep fighting their lives will never be impacted by you. The question is, are you going to be a champion and rise from the canvas or are you going to be a chump and stay down? I truly believe that if you are reading this book, you are going to be a champion and pull yourself up because you have a champion in you. Muhammad Ali said, "The canvas is no place for a champion."

I remember driving home that day and really not saying much to my friend Jim. I'm sure he was thinking to himself, I know the Patriots lost, but he is really taking it personally. While I sat in the passenger seat on a trip that seemed to take hours, I started to change my thinking and instead of thinking of all the reasons of why it wouldn't work, I started to think of the reasons why it would be okay. I started to think of the positive changes that would come into lives as a result of having a little one running around. The fun and excitement he or she would bring. I started to get excited about hearing hey Pepere, (*the French word for grandfather*). I decided to start focusing more on the solution instead of the problem. I realized that I needed to spend

90% percent of my time focusing on the solution and 10% of my time on the problem. Most people during their lifetime get it backward. They spend 90% of the time on the problem or the challenge and 10% of the time on the solution.

I asked Torie to meet me at the house so we could discuss the future and the challenges ahead. Making a decision to keep the child was not even a question, the only question was how we would make it work? I remember telling Torie that I was a single 45-year-old dad and I had no idea how we were going to do it and I had no plan - but we were going to do it. *"Everybody has a plan until they get punched in the face"* - Mike Tyson said that. Not everything that is easy is worth it but anything that is worth it is going to be hard and it was without a doubt going to be worth it. I knew we would come up with a plan because I had been working on myself by listening to the teachings of Jim Rohn, Les Brown, Zig Ziegler and several others. What I found was that although I didn't have a plan because I had been feeding my mind with positive things to help me grow, I had a plan in me. No matter how hard it was going to be, we were going to make it. As events or circumstances come into your life, you can't plan for the things that will happen to you but you can prepare yourself to deal with the circumstances by working everyday on your own personal development. Then, Torie said, "hey dad, can you do me a favor?" I said, "What would you like me to do Tor?" She said, "Can you tell my mother?" I replied with a chuckle "WHAT???- you want me to tell your mother?" I said, "Torie, I worked at a nightclub for six years where there were fights of most every night. Some nights those fights included knives and guns and other things that didn't scare me. I worked in a prison for 10 years where they were numerous fights and constant stress and that didn't scare me. But, to tell your mother our 15-year-old daughter was pregnant - that scares the heck out of me!" I said, "I'll help you with everything I can but you have to take some responsibility for what you did and you have to tell your mother you're pregnant. I want you to understand in life we can make our choices, but we can't always choose our consequences."

During the three days it took Torie the courage and strength to tell her mother, I began to assemble a team of people who would be able to help me because I knew I couldn't make it on my own. My team was made up of my dad, my mom, my brother Roger, my brother Robert, my sister Rita and my friends Lenny and Dona. These were the group of people who I was always surrounded by so I knew they would be there for me. Not one of them ever said that Tories life was ruined, that she would never make or that should not go through with it. No, they said we will do whatever ever they could to help me give Torie and the baby the best life they could possibly have.

 I want to take a look at your own life and see who you surround yourself with. Are they people who will support you, stand by you, encourage you, and bring out the best in you or are they people who will kick you when you're down, sucking the life out of you instead a breathing life into you? Most people want to see you get ahead in life as long as you don't get ahead of them; they either have to become more or choose to lead a life of mediocrity.

So many times I've heard people say I have a 1000 friends on Facebook, I have 5000 friends on Facebook and my question to is this - if you asked those 5000 friends if you could borrow some money because times are tough how many of these same friends would you have left? My guess is, not many. I have come to realize and I believe you will too, as you go through life and your circle of friends becomes smaller your life becomes bigger, when your friends become less, your life becomes more. Fewer friends fewer headaches.

When Torie finally had the courage to tell her mother I received a text message from her saying "I told her" to which my first thought was, now I'm scared. A few minutes after getting the text from Torie my phone rang and I didn't have to check the caller ID to see who it was because I already knew. I answered the phone and said hello to which I loudly heard, it true, is she pregnant? I said yes it is true and it was then that I got spoken to in a way I had never been spoken to before including the ten year period I was a prison guard. For anyone who may have only heard part of the conversation, they would have thought I was the one who got her pregnant. I responded by saying, hold on, hold on, I didn't get her pregnant, I just want to help her to which was responded to with more of the same type of language before being hung up on.

Torie later told me her mother responded to the news that she was pregnant by calling her a loser, she told her she had ruined her life, that her and her child would have nothing, that she was an embarrassment to my name and that she threw her life away. She went on to tell Torie that she wasn't having the baby and that she was getting an abortion and that she had no choice in what she was going to do. For Torie, it was the punch she never saw coming. To go to her mother and her stepfather, people who said how much they loved her and how great of a daughter she was, people who were always bragging about how great of a student she was and how great of an athlete she was but now when she really needed them they were not there for her.

I want you to take a look at your life and see if there was a time that you went to someone you loved and trusted and thought would always support you with an idea, a dream, or something you wanted to accomplish in life and they responded by telling you that you were not good enough, were not smart enough, didn't have the talent or abilities, or maybe even laughed at you and told you would never make it. For you maybe that was the punch you never saw coming. To be laughed at ridiculed and put down by someone who you trusted with your dreams.

Her mother called the abortion clinic and made Torie get on the phone to make the final appointment. Torie made the appointment knowing in her heart t she was not going to go through with it and that we already had a plan in place. Her mother drove her to the clinic on the day of the appointment and waited in the waiting room while Torie was being seen. While being spoken to by the nurse before the procedure Torie was asked the question, are you alright with this decision you are making to which she replied, it is not my decision. The nurse replied, what do you mean it is not your decision? Torie said you don't understand, my mother is in the waiting room, she is making me do this, it is her decision. The nurse asked her do you want to do this to which Torie again replied, no. I want to have this baby. I want to be responsible for the choice I made. Torie had to make the tough decision knowing that it would change her life forever. A tough decision is a tough decision not because we don't know the answer; a tough decision is a tough decision because we do know the answer, but we don't have the courage to do what we know so we do what we feel. Although Torie knew her decision would change her life forever she had the courage to make it. As you go through life and are working on becoming more, you will have to make choices you don't feel like making but know you have to make. I encourage you to make the tough decision and do what is right.

Torie then left the examination room headed straight out into the waiting room where her mother was sitting and informed her that she was not going through with the abortion. Her mother replied, what are you talking about are you saying you're not doing it? To which Torie replied, "NO!" I am not listening to you anymore, I am going to have this baby. Torie had to have the courage to stand up for herself and for what she believed in and not conform to her mother's wishes. *It was Thomas Watson that said "If you stand up and be counted from time to time you will get yourself knocked down but remember this, a man flattened by an opponent can get back up again, a man flattened by conformity stays down for good.* The only reward to conformity is that everybody likes you but yourself. *The opposite of courage isn't cowardice, it's conformity; even dead fish can go with the flow!*

If Torie would have conformed to her mother's wishes, the only people that would've been happy would have been the ones who wanted her to have the abortion. Torie would have had to live with the ghost of what could have been and what might've been for the rest of her life. Ask yourself, as I am going after my goals, my dreams, my purpose in life, my passion, am I going to have the courage to do as Torie did and say no I'm not listening to anyone trying to steal my dreams or am I going to conform to the wishes of others and abort my dreams, my goals, and my purpose in life and take them to the graveyard with me?

I believe the baby was given to Torie and only Torie could have given life to her child. If she would've conformed no lives would be changed by the baby that was in her. I believe if we abort our dreams, our goals, our purpose in life that only we can give life to - nobody else can give them life and we are depriving the world.

When Torie told some people that she was going to have the baby they laughed at her, they made fun of her, they even told her she was crazy. As you go after your dreams and your goals and share them with people, you too are going to get laughed at, made fun of and be told you are crazy; it is ok. Here it what I know, they told Bill Gates he was crazy and look at him today. They told the Wright Brothers they were crazy- look at air travel today. They told Thomas Edison he was crazy - look at light today. They told Steve Jobs he was crazy and this is what he said. *"Here's to the crazy ones, the misfits, the rebels, the troublemakers the round pegs in the square holes. The ones who see things differently. They're not fond of rules and they have no respect for the status quo. You can quote them, disagree with them, glorify or vilify them, but the only thing you can't do is ignore them - because they change things. They push the human race forward and while some may see them as the crazy ones, we see genius because the people who are crazy enough to think they can change the world, are the ones who do."*

Another thing most people do is crucify themselves between 2 thieves' regrets and memories of yesterday and fear of tomorrow; they die there. That's what happened to me. I remember being in the schoolyard around kids that I thought were my friends but when I would speak, I noticed nothing I said mattered. The kids would talk over me - like I wasn't even there. This continued through high school, and even into adulthood. Based on memories of the past, I made a decision that my words and my thoughts didn't matter with the exception of when I was a prison guard for 10 years. If I had to speak to a group of inmates they had to listen to me - if they didn't listen to me, I could lock them up! In the real world, I didn't have that option. While I was at a company event I was asked to speak. When I was approached by my mentor to give a talk, without hesitation, I said no because in my mind no one would listen to me. After hearing this, she said, "in order to grow, you must do things you don't want to do." After listening to her, I finally agreed and that day changed my life. Since that time, I have spoken in front of huge audiences, I have had the opportunity to share my story. In life, sometimes you have to believe in someone's belief in you until your belief in yourself kicks in. If you don't have the courage to take the necessary steps, if you don't have the courage to believe in yourself, to go after those dreams, to say to no to the naysayers - your dreams will forever die with you and you will never leave your mark. It has been said the only mark most people leave on this earth is the tombstone under which they are buried. Don't let that be you.

- THE FINAL ROUND

After finding out Torie was pregnant, I took her to her first doctor's appointment. Here's what the doctor said "Congratulations, you're pregnant, from this point on there will be no smoking, no drinking, no drugs". Fortunately, Torie didn't partake in any of these so this was not an issue for her but the reason the doctor tells the new mom this is because it's their job to protect the unborn child so the baby is not subjected to anything toxic. If we were to see a mom doing these things, we would want to say to her "why would you do that to your child, you are negatively impacting the life of your baby" STOP! Like a mother has to protect her unborn child, we have unborn dreams that are given to us yet we allow toxic thinking, toxic words, toxic people into our lives allowing it to abort our dreams. It our job to protect our dream just as it is the job of a mother to protect her unborn child. It is up to us to detoxify our lives even if it means letting go. Letting go of the past, letting go of bad habits and sometimes even letting go of people we love. Sometimes people come in to our lives for a season, a reason or a lifetime so don't keep them there toxifying your life for longer than they should be.

The next thing we have to realize is it's a process. The doctor doesn't say congratulations you are going to have a baby tomorrow. The birth of a child doesn't happen overnight. The woman has to prepare to be a mom, learn new skills, she has to make changes in her life to allow for the birth of her child. She has to go from becoming a woman to becoming a mom. Much like a mother preparing for birth, our dreams require that we go through the process, that we give our dreams time to grow, that we prepare for our dreams.

We have to learn to become more than we already are. We have to change our thinking, change what we say, change how we act, change what we do. We have to acquire new skills.

Another thing we have to realize as we fight for our dreams is that there are no short cuts. When a woman is pregnant with a child she can't speed up the process. But yet when we go after what we want in life sometimes we try to take the easy way or take a short cut if we can. There are no shortcuts. I remember certain people mentioning to Torie that there was a school for pregnant teenagers in the city where we lived where she could go at her own pace, stay home if she didn't feel good, take tests when she was ready. It was the easy way and she would not have to walk the halls of the big city high school.

I was thinking to myself why wasn't this offered to me when I was in school? I am so proud of Torie because without hesitation, she said, I am not taking the easy way out. I am going to go to the high school just like everyone else. I don't care if they laugh at me, I don't care if they tease me, I don't care what happens, I am going to the high school. Torie went through her normal high school, completed her sophomore year and had her baby shortly after.

It has been said that "Success never goes on sale, but most people spend their entire lives dickering over the price, never making the purchase. Pay full price, it's worth it.

I remember Torie starting to get excited about the new life she was bringing into the world and starting to picture what the baby would look like regardless of the fact that she was only a couple months pregnant and still had 7 months to go.

She began to think of names although she had no idea if it was going to be a boy or a girl. She started to look at baby clothes and baby furniture and what color she was going to paint the room. I even bought a new refrigerator and a new dishwasher. I didn't know why. I guess maybe I was thinking the baby would use it.

What I realized was that by Torie being excited and painting a vision of what her baby and her future would look like, I too began to get excited and be part the vision with her. As we go through the process of giving birth to our dream we need to do what Torie did. We need to see it finished long before it is. We have to have the vision of what it will look like and share it with the people who support us. So many times we share our dreams and our goals with the wrong people and they can make us blind.

Torie knew that if she shared her excitement and her vision with me, I would support her but on the other hand she couldn't share it with her mother. The outcome would not be the same. Protect your dream.

There were also some tough times for Torie during the nine months; it wasn't easy. I remember days she would wake up with morning sickness and still feeling tired. I remember days that she would call me from the bus to tell me she vomited on the way to school. There was a time when she slipped and fell on the ice. These times were tough for me to watch. To see my 15-year-old daughter going through this process was hard but I knew and she knew that no matter how tough it was she was going to make it and that it was worth it. There were times when she would say, I don't know how much longer I can take this dad and I would just keep saying, it will be worth it Tor, it will be worth it

There will be times that will get tough as you pursue your dreams and there will be days when you feel like giving up. Days when you feel like Torie did and you feel like you just can't do it anymore. I am telling you if you just hang on, if you just keep believing, if you just keep your dream in front of you, you too will see that it is worth it.

When that 9th month arrived after all that hard work, after all the sickness, after all the frustration, after all the ridicule, after all the changes Torie was ready to give birth to her baby. I remember her being in labor and working hard pushing and pushing and there was the one final hard push, Joel Osteen said "The hardest push comes right before the birth of a dream. On March 30th 2009, Torie gave birth to a beautiful baby girl, Savannah Paige. I remember hugging her and hearing her say with tears of joy in her eyes, we did it dad we did it. And all she wanted to do was hold her baby, kiss her baby and smell her baby's skin. None of the other stuff mattered, the tough times didn't matter, the ridicule from others didn't matter, the negative words from others didn't matter. All that mattered was that she accomplished what she wanted to do which was to have her baby. The same applies to you as you reach for your goals and your dreams. So when you finally accomplish what you set out to do you too can say, I did it, I made it. Can you imagine what it will feel like when you autograph your first book, cut your first album, start your nonprofit, open the door of your new business for the first time, losing that weight, or doing your first speech? Imagine!

In conclusion, I would like to share with you seven action steps that will help you achieve your dreams:

Step 1: Start from where you are. Don't wait for things to be perfect because they never will be. I know when the doctor told Torie she was pregnant she couldn't say, well can you put it off for a few weeks so I can get ready? Start right now, where you are and with what you have. *Jim Rohn said, go outside pick up a rock, throw it up in the air and wherever it lands, start there."*

Step 2: Trust the process. You don't have to try to figure it all out. Just know in your heart that things will work out. Most people never succeed in life because they spend more time studying the roots of the tree instead of just picking the fruit. Pick the fruit.

Step 3: Remember you are enough. You don't have to be someone else. You have everything you need to get started. You have what it takes. If you didn't have what it takes the dream wouldn't be given to you.

Step 4: Invest in yourself. Invest in your health, invest in your mind. It is sad, but we live in a world where the smartphones are getting smarter and people are getting dumber. Most people spend more time and money going to watch other people live their dreams than they do working on their own dreams. What they don't realize is that the athletes, the musicians and other talented people they are going to watch spent more time working on their dreams than watching others live theirs. Invest in yourself.

Step 5: Never lose sight of your dream. One day my wife Julie brought home some new bones for our dog Claire and placed them on the top back of her cage where she couldn't reach them. Claire knowing that they were there cried for them and stood on her back legs begging for them. I told Julie to get her the old bone she had been chewing on. A bone that she would not let us touch prior to the purchase of the new bones. She would hide with it so we wouldn't bother her. Julie got the old bone but Claire wanted nothing to do with it, all she wanted was the new bone. After a few minutes, I moved the bag of bones to a shelf where she couldn't see them but saw me put them there. She continued to stand on her back legs begging for the bone for a few minutes even though she couldn't see them. After a little bit, I went to see if she was still begging for the bones but she was gone. I soon found her hiding in a room chewing on her old bone and when I went to take it she took it and walked away. So many times when we get a new dream, find a new purpose in life or even a new relationship we get excited and we leave the past behind us in order to pursue what is new.

But, as time goes on sometimes our vision gets a little blurry and our dream, our goal, our purpose or even the relationship becomes unclear and maybe even out of sight. Like Claire, we continue for a short time pursuing it even if we can't see it but eventually we give up and go back to what we know, what is comfortable, what is routine and we just want to be left alone, just like Claire went back to chewing her old bone. I want you right now to decide today you are going to BURY THE BONE and go after whatever it is you want even when you can't see it. BURY THE BONE.

Step 6: Go the distance. If a fighter is ready for a fight he doesn't train for a 3 round fight if it is a 12 round fight. No, he trains for a 20 round fight so he can go the distance. In the movie Rocky, Mickey says it best:

For a 45-minute fight, you gotta train hard for 45,000 minutes. 45,000! That's ten weeks, that's ten hours a day, ya listenin'? And you ain't even trained one!

Most people give up before they start. Go the distance.

Step 7: See who you are surrounded by. Are they bringing you up or dragging you down? Are they going your way or in your way. Some people you are going to have to count on some you are going to have to count out.

Listen to what you are listening to. Is it making you better or making you bitter? Is what you are listening to feeding your mind or starving your mind? Remember: It is not garbage in, garbage out. It is, garbage in, garbage stays in until you push it out.

Listen to what you are saying that other people are listening to. Are your words lifting them up or dragging them down? Remember if something is being learned by what you are saying, you are teaching.

No one made me more aware than that than my 4-year-old granddaughter Savannah. I am constantly studying quotes and repeating them over and over again never thinking that my granddaughter Savannah was listening and then one day while driving in the car she started to recite a quote I had been studying. I never realized she was listening and that I was teaching. I said, Savannah, do you know the whole quote? She said yes pep - I know the whole thing.

This is what she said:

If you want a thing bad enough to go out and fight for it, to work day and night for it, to give up your time, your peace and sleep for it... if all that you dream and scheme is about it ...and life seems useless and worthless without it... if you gladly sweat for it and fret for it and plan for it and lose all your terror of the opposition for it...if you simply go after that thing that you want with all your capacity, strength and sagacity, faith hope and confidence and stern pertinacity...if neither cold, poverty, famine, nor gout, sickness nor pain, of body and brain, can keep you away from the thing that you want...if dogged and grim you beseech and beset it, with the help of God, YOU WILL GET IT!

You have a Champion in you!

PH: 508-965-4288
EMAIL: rolandmannyspeaks@gmail.com

CREATING A QUANTUM SHIFT

Carlenia Springer

Bio

Dr. Carlenia Springer, creator of DESTINY EMBRACED teaches a practical spirituality, she is a Visionary, Entrepreneur, Spiritual Teacher, Speaker, Certified Coach and Author, who supports conscious women entrepreneurs in leveraging their intuitive nature in life and business. DESTINY EMBRACED is a place for women who want to build a better world, unleash their voices and communicate their vision and passion through their businesses. Carlenia is passionate about supporting parents in recognizing the intuitive abilities of their children and giving them space to discover soul's purpose for their lives. She holds an honorary doctorate from Global Oved Dei Seminary and University and a BA in Psychology from University of Maryland. Her training includes 2 years with Dr. Iyanla

Vanzant at Inner Visions Institute of Spiritual Development, 2 years studying with Sobonfu Some, in Ritual Healing Village, learning the ancient ways of being in community, she studied with Master Coach Ron Davis at Ascend Spiritual Flight Academy and 5 years with Rev. Israel Malik Esters of World Awakening Universal Church of Christ.

You may contact her at carlenia@destinyembraced.org or on Facebook.com/DestinyEmbracedHome.

I knew that everywhere I looked a message was left for me from those who guided from beyond the veil. Another song was coming through "everything's not what it seems, there's a stronger force behind the scenes..." they always let me know that they saw me and I mattered. It was years before I realized that the songs 'randomly' popping in my mind were not random at all. They always spoke to what was going on with me in the moment or what was about to happen. The unusual thing about these songs, were they were never songs I would normally sing or hear in my mind. Sometimes they were hymns or other religious songs I hadn't heard or thought about in years and other times they were secular songs but not the ones I would just turn on the radio and expect to hear.

It was these glimpses into a reality not explained by my upbringing that fascinated me from a child. "Who am I? What am I? Where did I come from?" I remember gazing into the night sky surveying the twinkling lights with an unexplainable longing, a knowing that I was from out there somewhere, but where? And how did I get here? I was told that god made us, but where did god come from? He had to come from somewhere. The answers were unsatisfying to me as a child and instinctively I knew that even though the adults in my life meant well, they didn't have the answers either. The mystery, the call of the deep, was always there, right below the surface waiting to break through.

Facing a painful childhood of survival from the moment I can remember myself, I truly believed with everything in me that I had no creativity and no personality. Any expression of individuality was just about obliterated by my relationship with my mom. My life had become one big reaction to her long before I knew myself. My earliest memories of my mom are where she described herself as an angry, frustrated young mother unleashing that anger on me. By the time I heard this I was already well trained and conditioned subconsciously to fear her and fear for my personal safety and well-being.

My conditioning was so thorough, I always found myself unable to make the simplest decisions. I never trusted my choices. I felt my essence being violently obliterated. I spent my entire childhood just trying to be silent and respectful, not saying or doing anything to get in trouble or upset my mom.

In hindsight it's clear why I experienced myself as starving for love and true companionship, and feeling helpless to do anything about it. I developed a strong belief that I couldn't survive without someone else being there. Burned into my subconscious memory was a belief that I wasn't worth living. These experiences set up devastating patterns in my relationships. The pattern would play out in my first marriage with verbal and physical violence and in my second marriage with the violence of deafening silence. In many different ways I experienced 'I don't hear you, I don't see you, who you are doesn't matter.'

I had no understanding of the catastrophic psychological damage I suffered as a child. I just knew it as my life. I hated it and thought I hated my mom for a long time. I learned to survive in an environment where I felt unloved and unsafe. I was always told I was loved and it confused me, because I believed it.

Many years later while sitting in a spiritual training class at Inner Visions I would hear a song that opened my heart to the little girl inside who thought she had lost so much that she no longer trusted anyone in her world, not even god.

"How could anyone ever tell you, you were anything less than beautiful? How could anyone ever tell you, you were less than whole? How could anyone ever fail to notice that your loving is a miracle, how deeply you're connected to my soul?"

The tears began flowing. I never thought of myself as beautiful. I knew my heart was so full of love but I had no idea what to do with that love, and I didn't feel like anyone noticed me or my love. For the first time in my life I recognized a little girl so afraid and so scared she needed to build thick fortresses around her heart, determined that no one else would ever hurt or harm her again. She didn't know those fortresses designed to protect her were also blocking her from giving and receiving love. I tried being brave, I tried acting like I didn't care, but the truth was I wasn't brave at all and I felt everything, every emotion, my own and others very deeply. Too much pain and no idea what to do with it, so from an early age I determined that no matter how hard I was hit or beaten physically as a child or emotionally I would show no weakness or vulnerability.

My first marriage had been a walk in total darkness. I was in my second marriage and it wasn't working. For the past 7 years I had been married to a nice, easygoing, mild-mannered man who had gotten along pretty well with my two children until recently, when he completely lost it in a rage that broke the relationship between him and my daughter.

Up until this point I had convinced myself that this time around my marriage was different than before. The strange thing was I still felt isolated and in my own world, unable to connect with myself or the man I loved. I had made myself believe that this time was so much better. I had longed for peace. I had longed for serenity and someone to share it with. Yet I still found myself with someone who was physically there and emotionally unavailable. He was unable to express anything much beyond anger and laughter every now and then. Perhaps with another person he would be more open and expressive I told myself. This life was comfortable at some level and I still had that niggling feeling I could experience so much more.

I wanted to live and I was dying inside. My husband had long since moved into his own world, seemingly content to live this drab, uninteresting, mundane existence for the rest of his life. I felt helpless to do anything about it. My desire to fight was very low. Fight for what? I was too paralyzed.

I had known him for 10 years and still couldn't figure him out. I was tired of running. Seven years was enough. Everywhere I looked there was some unfinished project he had started and couldn't complete for countless reasons. I was tired and ready to move, unwilling to live in this messed up but 'comfortable' situation anymore.

I believed in my heart that we were given this life to live as if it were our last. He was opposite, to him that was crazy, irresponsible and uncaring of the others in your life. He had to figure it out, get comfortable with it and be sure. I was spontaneous, inhibited but desperately wanting to break free. I thought that scared him and I felt for him and hoped one day he could be free of his inhibitions. I was no longer willing to put my dreams on hold, bury my dreams and aspirations for anyone else in my life. I was no longer going to use the excuse of 'my husband' wouldn't like that.

My soul longed to express and experience life, to taste it, smell it, embrace it, love it and be made love to by the essence of life. My soul was awakening and coming to life. I breathed in the mystery of my being and the world in which I had come alive. I made a decision to embrace everything mystical & unique about myself. I wasn't going to hide anymore. I decided that I was going to become a healthy, wealthy and sensuous size 8 woman, who was a sought after speaker, visionary, healer, spiritual teacher and world traveler. What I envisioned filled me with immense joy.

As I drifted back to my current reality from the place I knew I would be, I understood that everything familiar would be gone and I didn't have to know what would happen, I had already seen it. I knew that when the time came I would instinctively know what to do and do it with ease. I had learned how to take one step at a time. I recalled the many times in life when angels appeared to clear a path before me. It was happening again and this time I knew it had already been planned and all I had to do was follow.

This time I would do it differently and I would choose not to fight or waiver. I would choose to be obedient to my spirit. This way of being was new but I had always walked with my guidance. My guidance came in different ways sometimes I would just know something, unsure really of how I knew it. Other times I would be given insight into situations through dreams, I knew these were not ordinary dreams.

I was receiving messages during dream-time. I knew that when I saw certain numbers and synchronicities that occurred at the same time there were no such things as happenstance and I was receiving a message to either move on or pay attention. I knew when I thought of someone that transitioned, there was a message for me or someone close to them. I knew I had to follow those messages and although at times my mind would have liked for me to believe that I was making it up, those messages undeniably made a difference in other people's lives.

I knew I could see spirit and even the spirit of those still here. I knew my gifts were passed down through the generations and that my grandmother has the gift and my grandfather had it also. I knew my abilities were growing as my memory grew stronger day by day. I knew that when talking to someone, messages would spontaneously come through for them. I knew there were people in my world who were part of my soul group and had agreed to work with me.

I knew I had premonitions and could interpret other people's dreams. I knew that by listening to my instincts and acting upon it I could save myself heartache. I knew I carried a tremendous love in my heart that could dissolve people's pain and bring them back into balance. I knew I could send love and melt hearts that erected barriers. I knew that by bringing my light to what I desired I could have it. I knew that my power lay within and miracles occurred when I went inside my mind to effect outer change and transformation. I knew my voice was clear and powerful. I knew physical healing could occur by my touch. I knew that by acknowledging these and so much more as my gifts that I would give others permission to embrace their gifts.

I had no idea what it would take for me to get to the other side. What I knew was that I had enough of the pain of disconnection. Moving through the pain was teaching me how to shift and go with the flow. Deep within I knew the countdown had begun and I was ok. I would take it one step at a time. I understood "*Intimacy is where we are willing to move so deeply into love that the demons do not deter us from our conviction to make it through to the light.*" I was willing to walk into the darkness to get to the light. I had no idea of the darkness to come and that I would have to call on everything I had learned up until that point to move me through the darkness and embrace my destiny.

I remained in my marriage for another 6 years, learning, growing and expanding. I understood that what we see in our relationships and in our experience is a projection of deep seeded beliefs and I was determined to create harmony in my marriage and release the anger, blame and unforgiveness. But, the more I grew and began taking responsibility for my experiences, the farther apart we grew. I recall a day when I sat in my spiritual class and whatever I heard that day expanded my understanding exponentially and I knew my husband couldn't take that journey.

My husband left the day of my childhood friend's funeral. As we were getting ready to leave the house to go to the church he turned and quietly said I'm leaving. I didn't understand what he was saying at first. I wasn't expecting it, not then. I asked him why he would wait until the day I was burying my friend, couldn't he have said this before or after the funeral? He didn't answer. He just asked why I was looking at him like that, I asked like what, he said like he had done something wrong.

In that moment I knew I couldn't go down that road, not today, not ever. I knew where that path led. I wasn't prepared for that level of grief, my heart couldn't take it and that is where my practice of being present and shifting my attention from the past or future into the present moment was tested. I was scared. I couldn't cry because I knew I would lose it and I needed to maintain composure for my kids. Everything I knew was tested that year, all my emotions were put through the wringer and the only thing that supported me in keeping my sanity was a mental discipline of shifting my attention into the present moment and reminding myself that although I felt the pain, who I was as spirit was untouched and I was ok. It was a battle and I was in a fight for control of my mind.

DESTINY EMBRACED

It would be another 3 years before my divorce would be finalized. Almost every day that first year was a mental battle not to allow my emotions to dominate. There were times I felt I had run 5 miles and hadn't moved anything but my thoughts. Every time I was hit with sadness I went to 'work' – 'I know I'm feeling the effects of being sad but I'm spirit and spirit isn't sad.' I would do that countless times in an hour, in half an hour, in 15-minutes, whenever it hit me.

I would remind myself that 'everything is consciousness', nothing is happening outside of me, nothing. Everything I think about what I see, hear and feel is being generated from a deeper level of my mind. I worked with being 100% responsible for everything in my life. It was an epic fight-a moment-to-moment battle to regain territory and take back control of my mind. What I discovered later was a depth of emotional stability I didn't know I had. There were times I faced situations that would have taken me out emotionally for 2 or 3 months and after 2 days I didn't feel anything. I didn't know what to make of it at first but after a few times I realized that something deep within my mind had shifted. It was then I recognized the value of meditation. In meditation I was working things out at levels of which I was unaware.

During that time my intuitive abilities were greatly heightened and yet I couldn't recognize it. I was too busy fighting. I knew things I had no logical way of knowing and often believed it was just my own thoughts. Almost 6 months to the day he left, my husband's mom died unexpectedly. 4 months later my friend Natacha was in my home, we were standing in my kitchen when she mentioned a pulling sensation on her left ear. I found it strange and told her that earlier in the year my daughter was in the dining room and mentioned a pulling sensation on her ear, she was thinking very strongly about my grandmother and had taken a picture of herself at the same time. In the picture was a large golden circle of light right next to her. The sun wasn't shining through the window and we didn't know what it was. She got scared and deleted it shortly afterwards.

Then, I pointed to a photograph on the mantle and told Natacha that was a picture of my husband's mom and dad. "Oh, I felt something from the woman but not from the man," she said.

"What did you say?" I asked surprised at her comment. "What do you mean?"

"When I walked in here, I felt the pulling sensation on my ear and connected it to her." I told Natacha about my husband's mom passing but that was the first time she was in my home so she didn't know who they were and had never met my husband. Then she began speaking, "she wants them to tell the dad to get his papers in order, he has to do it now or all hell will break out in the village, she doesn't want to tell me what it's about but she's insisting he needs to do it now." There was a strong sense of urgency in Natacha's voice and I stood there absolutely stunned.

I didn't know she had this kind of ability. I had never seen anything like it in my life and what was more shocking was the information. I knew nothing about what she shared. My husband never talked about his family, not even the usual everyday conversation. I tried telling him what Natacha had said and he dismissed me outright. He said he didn't believe in those things, she didn't know what she was talking about and his dad's papers were in order. When I told Natacha she began speaking again as if relaying an even stronger message from the mom. I said I would call his younger brother who lived in Florida, he was the most open minded of all of them and that would be the best I could do.

I called his brother, shared the information and immediately there was a sigh and silence on the other end of the line, then he said 'that's the one thing none of us want to do, we don't want our dad to think we want his money." He thanked me and said he would handle it.

I was rendered speechless. I believed my husband, even though I knew what I saw and experienced. I was so used to not trusting myself and accepting other people's opinion over my own, it was a pattern of self-abandonment. Through my connection to Natacha I slowly began realizing I was accessing similar information but it was coming through a thick cloud and I couldn't decipher the information from my own thoughts. I had dreams of my husband's mom and every time I dreamed my daughter would have a dream that was different but the energy was similar.

I remember my daughter waking up one morning extremely excited "I just dreamed about his mom and she was so happy and she told me I had to tell you, I think she wanted me to share this joy with you. I ran around the corner to tell you and I told you, but it was like I woke up from a dream inside a dream and now this is the second time I'm telling you!"

My eyes were barely open as I stretched my arm across the bed and said, 'my goodness you've made contact.' My fingers touched something small and hard, 'what is this?' I opened my eyes to see what I had touched, it was 2 very dry and shriveled contact lenses. 'What in the world is going on? What are your contact lenses doing here? I asked my daughter. "I don't know."

"Get a piece of paper and write that dream down and my response to you and tape these contact lenses to the paper so we don't ever dismiss this experience." My eyes were being opened to other levels of reality. I began to understand that things are not as they appear, we are connected to everyone and everything and love truly never dies. What dies are parts of us when we lose a loved one and we believe the connection is gone with the exception of our memories. The pain and disconnection that comes with our belief in death is the biggest lie we've bought into. We associate ourselves with the body and when the body is gone we believe the person is gone.

My experiences with the loss of my friend, my husband's leaving and the connection with his mother left me with an innate understanding that we are all deeply connected and communicating all the time. Whether or not we are aware of the connection is a function of how awake we are to our true nature as spirit. Over that year my husband continuously expressed surprise at what I knew about his situation and circumstances after he left. His communication with me never changed but my communication with myself and acknowledgement that when I thought of someone it wasn't happenstance allowed me to access and act on information I was receiving.

My world began opening as I was pulled by the synchronicity of my experiences and this ability to see an underlying pattern to reality that wasn't readily apparent on the surface. In February of the following year I connected with an old friend, we began dating and I experienced the most expansive, connected, conscious relationship of my life. We traveled overseas and locally and it was like a love letter from the Universe saying, you have much further to go but we want to show you what life is going to be like on the other side.

We spoke each other's language and eerily our lives mirrored each other although we had taken different paths. Through the lessons we learned, the appreciation for ourselves, and the standards we set – some things were no longer an option. We had raised the bar and no matter what we knew we would never ever go back to where we had come from. We prayed together, we meditated together, if something upset one of us the other was calm and could listen from a space of love and know that ultimately the pain being triggered had everything to do with our past experience and not us. We were committed to being present and taking life one moment at a time. We were aware of our fears and weaknesses and understood the ways they would show up in our communication.

I was committed to loving myself and communicating even when it was challenging. I was committed to taking on my inner conversation and observing how it showed up in my relationship and still being 100% responsible for my results. This relationship was proof positive that I had crossed a threshold and it was never ever about the other person it was about me learning, growing, expanding, discovering, accepting and loving all of me. Was there fear? Absolutely! But every time I faced my fear and had a conversation where I normally would have shrunk back into my shell I experienced a greater opening and a greater level of understanding and intimacy with myself and in my relationship.

I was proving to myself that things were not as they appeared and anytime I wanted to effect outer change in my world I had to go inside, discover where I was doing the thing I wanted others to change and when I shifted they would automatically shift. They would either rise to the occasion or fall out of my life. I discovered the real magic was inside of me. I didn't have to trust anybody as long as I trusted myself, everything was fine. As long as I remained in integrity with me I would know what I needed to know, when I needed to know it.

I don't know where you are right now but if what I've said is resonating and you find yourself with your back against the wall not knowing where to turn, I want you to know that there is a way out. You see, in one of my darkest moments Spirit said to me, you're not looking for a way out, you're looking for a way into the heart of who you are. When you discover who you are, what you think of as the way out will be made plain.

I couldn't do this by myself. I had a lot of spiritual training and little integration. I had a mentor who taught me how to use my mind and work with spiritual principles. He taught me there was no substitute for meditation, just as there was no substitute for practice, discipline, focus and commitment. There were times when I couldn't see my way and he shone light so I could continue to move. With all of his guidance if I didn't put in the work I wouldn't have produced the results. I was hungry, my life had to change, it wasn't an option.

So if you find yourself in a place no longer acceptable to you and you've made the decision that you need a quantum shift in your life and you need it now, here are 7 steps you can implement to get on the right track.

Practice having a clear picture in your mind daily. Take a trip in your imagination and visit a version of yourself that has already mastered the very challenge you're experiencing and learn from them. Whatever action you can take begin it now and be committed to taking action every day until you're shown what to do next.

Feed your mind daily. Listen as often as you can each day to someone who inspires you to live a more expansive life, play a bigger game and take action towards your dreams. Listen continuously for 2 weeks understanding the more you listen, the more you will embody the speaker's energy. Play it on repeat at night when you go to sleep. Your outlook on life will begin to transform.

Strengthen your intuition daily. Use a personal development book and upon waking ask Spirit "where should I put my attention today?" Open the book without looking and point. Read the first 3 sentences and where ever you are directed place your attention right there. Throughout your day pay attention to whether your mind is wandering to past or future challenges or if you are present in the moment.

- *__Practice silence.__* Meditate or sit in the silence for at least 15 minutes daily. For two minutes after meditation, write any new awareness, impressions or feelings that arise.

- *__Invest in yourself__*. What you have learned has brought you to where you are. In order to get to the next level you're going to have to surround yourself with minds more brilliant and accomplished and learn from them. I've spent tens of thousands of dollars on personal development and spiritual training. There is no other way but to invest time, money and energy into improving yourself.

- *__Work 1-on-1 with a coach or mentor__*. You will literally collapse time frames around reaching your goals. This is the fastest way to make measurable progress if you're willing to do what they say so you can achieve a higher level of success.

- *__Practice being a contribution__*. Find a way to give without expectation of something in return. That's how I met my mentor. I didn't have lots of money so I found a national philanthropy project called 'Little Dresses for Africa' and I created a local group of women in my community to participate. One day my mentor, who was teaching next door, introduced himself to me. I had no idea it was a divine appointment that would lead to my transformation.

Brigitte Nicole said "You will experience true freedom when you let go of what is hurting your heart and soul." You are a creator. Your gifts were meant to be given, the path you've come through is so you'll be able to help others. You are destined for greatness. When you embrace your DESTINY you will give from your overflow. Your gifts will make a way for you. Your needs will be met and many others blessed because you said YES to your ASSIGNMENT and YES to your LIFE!

I AM A TESTIMONY

John McClung Jr.

Mr. John McClung Jr. is Founder / CEO of 'I AM A TESTIMONY' Clothing Collection. Mr. John McClung currently resides in Las Cruces, New Mexico by way of Long Beach, Ca. He is the Elder son of the late Pastor John E. McClung Sr. former Pastor of Living Word Missionary Baptist Church in Long Beach, Ca. He is a graduate of University of Phoenix with three degrees, MBA in Bus. Man, BS/BA in Business. He is a Motivational speaker, founding member of Men Of Vision and is a member of the Sensational Speakers Syndicate as well as Black Belt Speakers.

He is the Best Selling Co-Author of the book "I AM A TESTIMONY"- Inside the relationship Mind of a P.K. and topic speaker of "IT'S YOUR TIME TO FLY" How to take flight and live your dreams. He was Inspired to create a Christian Clothing line that expresses the testimony that each of us has in our lives. The foundation of this mission is based on, John 3:33, KJV 'He that hath received his 'Testimony' hath set to his seal that God is true. "

John can be reached by email: iamatestimony@yahoo.com, website: www.testimonyiam.com. His Facebook page: John McClung Jr., Twitter: @testimonyiam also on LinkedIn. And Facebook fan page: I Am A Testimony

Life leaves its landmarks. In October of 1980 I set out on my own to conquer the world, but I really was just trying to leave home and venture out on my own. I wanted to make my mark on the world and although I was a 18 year old ambitious young man, I had big hopes and aspirations as well as dreams.

I grew up in a home full of love, closeness, spirituality and discipline. You see, I grew up in the home of a minister and there were so many days I was reminded of that. I am not saying that growing up as a preacher's kid was bad, but it certainly was not easy. There were many days that often reminded me of the things I thought I missed and I certainly thought I was supposed to be bad because I always heard that, 'we were the worst kids in the world'.

There were times that I didn't think I could ever be a good kid, because of what I had heard and I often wondered were my friends being told the same thing. I did understand that these words were coming from other people, my parents never called us the worst kids in the world and that was some comfort, but when we stepped outside of the house it was a different world.

When I decided to leave home 3 months after I graduated I wasn't just leaving the family, or friends or the neighborhood, I was leaving behind an identity that wasn't for me. When you grow up in a prominent minister's home, you can lose your identity, for that fact you can lose your identity in any home if you allow it to happen. Having a father who was faithful to God and his ministry placed an added amount of pressure on others to label me as 'the one' to be like my father, I was supposed to be the preacher.

Well, needless to say as a young kid I didn't know what or who I was going to be because it had somewhat by others been decided for me, my voice was gone…..

I often wondered how many other people had loss their voice because someone had already identified who they were going to be and they never really had a chance to realize their own potential or speak to who it was they wanted to be. I knew that was not how I saw my life and it was a struggle to separate who others wanted me to be and who I was going to be. I can't say I remember my father ever saying he wanted me to be like him, but I guess he didn't need too, others were doing it for him.

It was difficult working in the shadows of a God fearing man and wanting to have a voice that screamed, 'I just want to be me!' Have you ever just wanted to scream and let the world know, 'I am not like anyone else?' And believe me, being like my father was not a bad thing, but not being me was the thing that I could not get over. Some may have believed I was fighting the inevitable. You see, I had some of the traits of a servant's heart and the ability to teach, I got it honest, just like any other kid who watched their parents closely you just pick up some things that work for you even though they might not be you.

At 18, I thought I was ready to leave the nest, the confines of a warm and loving home, a mother who thought the world of her oldest son and wanted so much to have the best for me in everything and a father who would have loved to have me follow in his footsteps. I knew that would make him proud! But, that would have made him proud, what about me?

I saw so many others who decided to listen to the people they were surrounded by and not become the person they were supposed to be. I watched many waste their talents, gifts and abilities listening to others. I couldn't see how they could let their life go to waste or be a victim of what others wanted for them when they wanted something else and was too afraid to go and get it, too afraid to step out an find their own identity, kick the box of being a duplicate instead of being the unique person God intended them to be, that was not going to happen to me.

I was fortunate to know early in life that despite what others said I would be, I knew, that despite the words that were being spoken into my life, there was a different plan for me, there was different path, a different dream, a different reason to live. I knew that I had some traits that would allow me to help others in my own way, speak in to others in my own way and change lives for the better, including mine. I didn't know how long it would take, but I knew that is what I was supposed to do.

When I thought about leaving, I remembered all those days I had to go to church, it was all I knew. Some days as a little kid we were the church. I remembered all the fun I missed out on, some of the places we could not go, things I could not participate in, it seems like I had a tough childhood, in some sense yes, but in other ways no. I just wanted to have the ability of not being judged, growing up with all eyes on your every move, that is some crazy pressure for a kid! But I didn't choose the life, my parents did and these were some of the challenges that came with that decision.

The difficult part of choosing to venture out on your own is the unknown. I really had no idea what purpose was, I wasn't listening to any books or tapes, going to seminars, or motivational speeches except the ones I heard every week from my father. I was just running from everything that was not me, I was running from what I thought was the inability to choose who I wanted to be, I was running from the safety of wisdom and experience, heck, I was just running.

Do you know what that is like? Can you identify with just running? Maybe from your past, or from a bad relationship, broken home, bad marriage, crazy job, and you have no idea where you are going. I know I am not by myself when I speak about this, but that is how I felt. It was a transition time that I had to face and as bad and my parents wanted me to stay, as I sat across from them and told them I wanted to leave and go my own way.

I used school as my shelter for leaving but I knew I wanted a taste of the world, my own experiences, my own failures, my own challenges, my own obstacles as well as my own successes. I wanted to prove that I didn't have to be like someone else to succeed, although I still wanted them to be proud of me, I had to let them see their son needed his own space. Do you need your own space? It doesn't have to be hidden in leaving home, it could be you need some breathing room; you need to follow your dreams act on your vision, pursue your own goals, whatever it is, only you know.

I wanted to create experiences that would help me share with others. There was something in me saying, you have something unique and you need to find it no matter how long it takes. Was it tough out there, heck yeah! Did I run into things I wasn't prepared for and had to figure it out, you better believe it, did life knock me down and say to me, 'what you gonna' do?' Absolutely! And I know if you are reading this, it has done the same thing to you as well, it's just the way life is.

I remember telling myself, 'all that you do is not just for you and it is not for everybody, but if you can help somebody, then it will eventually affect everybody' and so my goal was to take this journey as a young man and grow into a man that could make an impact on others by sharing the experiences that help me grow into someone that they could identify with. Did life take some things from me? Yes it did! You see, leaving home and making it this far didn't keep me from getting scars, it didn't keep me from losing jobs, it didn't keep from losing a home or being homeless, it didn't keep me from not having any money and knowing where my next meal was coming from, it didn't have mercy on me when I was crying out for help, No! Life just kept on teaching me lessons, the kind of lessons that helped me learn to see that I needed to have a plan, I needed to have some type of strategy that would get me through. And the tough part was, where do I start?

And I just bet that that life has given you some type of fight, it has you in the ring and you are taking some punches that you did not see coming, you have had some blows that caught you off guard and you may even have had to take a standing eight count because those punches left you in a daze! Well, I understand and you don't have to be one who can't fight back, or not have a game plan to get through the rounds. You can go back to your corner, pull yourself together, listen to your trainer and come back out swinging like I did.

Yeah, that 18 year old teenager, had to go through some difficult rounds, had to take some significant blows, even having to deal with the loss of the most influential man in his life. You see growing up is not easy to do, because some may think it's based on age, No! Experience has taught me, it is those very things that provide the lessons that you can help someone else with. You see unless you have been in a fight, you can't become a champion and the only the only way you can share your Testimony is if you have gone through a test.

If you see yourself in these words, if you have identified with not having a voice of your own, if you have been one who has been beat up by life, keep reading! I am going to share some things that helped me get to where I am today. I want to share some principles that have been a part of me learning how to live my dream, how to shape my life and how to impact the lives I have had the opportunity of crossing during this journey. I had no idea the road I would be taken down, but today I understand why I was supposed to leave the comforts of home and journey down this path towards my destiny.

I wondered what it would be like when I had a chance for my voice to be heard, to share my experiences, my wisdom and pour into the life of others. I no longer have to wonder because I am doing just that! And as you continue to read, I want to share just a few principles that guided my life and helped me to see the dreams I thought that were never possible become a reality. You see if you are anything like me, and you are a dreamer, you need to know that Dreams can come true!

Before leaving home, my father gave me some advice and he would always give me one word whenever I called him. It didn't have to be a long drawn out conversation, he wasn't going to do that, he was just going to lay on my heart and mind a word that would take me through the next few weeks. So, I am going to share a few things from the word he gave me and then I am going to share some principles that helped me get through some difficult challenges, tough times and create a mindset, that there was nothing I could not accomplish.

I know you are wondering, what is the word he is going to share that can help me in my life? Well the word is DESIRE, A word I am sure you have heard before. The next few minutes of reading I want to provide some definition to this word that shaped my life and helped me go through every Test and become a Testimony.

You see, the word Desire means: To wish or Long for, to want, request or petition. Have you when reading this definition felt any of these things? I know I did and I begin to dig a little deeper and find out why my dad chose this word that would change my life in so many ways. Here is what I learned, that Desire is what gets you up off the couch, it is what makes you dream, it is what keeps you going.

One of my favorite books, well really my favorite book, says 'Delight thyself in the Lord and he shall give thee the Desires of thine heart'. Now Delight means to pamper so you have to learn how to pamper your Dreams, Purpose and Desires.

I had heard this on so many occasions and I am sure you probably have as well, but I want to shed a totally different light on this as you read further. What Desire do you have for yourself? What Desire have you not accomplished? What Desire if accomplished would totally change your life?

I worked for an Airlines and I had the opportunity to work out on the runway and I had the chance to learn some lessons on the runway that were applicable to life and the Desires we have for our life. I watched so many people live their travel Desire when they got on those planes. But, here is something you may have never known, the instrument used to move the plane from the gate on to the runway. This instrument needed to be attached to the plane in order for the plane to be given the all go sign and pushed back from the gate and on to the runway so it can prepare to take off- That tool used was called a TUG.

One of the life lessons learned on that runway was that everyone who desires to have anything in life first has to have a Tug. I understood that there has to be a tug of some sort for you to go after the desires of your heart. So, what is tugging at you to do what it is you want to do? Is that new job tugging at you, what about writing that new book or becoming a teacher, is it that new relationship you want to start or getting on stage to sing that new song? Understand and know, there is a Tug on your life that wants you to have the Desires of your heart.

When you have a Tug on your life, you must understand the **first** thing:

You must be Desire Specific – What do I mean by that? Glad you asked. When you begin to go after your desires, your dreams your vision, when you know and understand that there is a tug on you to do something, you must be very specific about it. You need to be very clear before you begin to chase after it. This is a principle I didn't really get until later, but I want you to get it now, 'That which you are specific about, will come about.' You must and again, I say must have clarity about what it is you want for your life. You cannot just make a decision and not have full understanding of why you are doing it. Your specific decision must change a life, help a life and add value to a life.

Second, before an individual decides to go to the airport and get on a flight, there is some strategy involved. You don't just pick any place to go, you have a desire to go somewhere specific, right and then you create a strategy to get there, this is called being Desire Strategic. There is strategy to the Desire you have for yourself. There are steps you need to take to be successful. Before you decided to move forward on your purpose or journey, you need to make sure you have a plan. Now, when I left home I didn't quite have a plan and some of my failures proved it. But from those non planned lessons, I quickly learned that if I was going to be able to have my tug get me on to the runway, I needed to make sure I had a good flight plan. That plan can evolve over time, but be sure that you have one.

The **third** thing I want to share about desire, is that you must be strong about the choices you make for your life, in other words you must be Desire strong. You need to have such conviction about what you want to do in life, that you eat, sleep, drink and breathe it every day. Being Desire strong means, that everything about you will stand strong for what you believe for yourself, that you cannot be moved, your Desire is so strong that it can stand any test. Do you have a desire for your life that strong? Do you see yourself doing what you want to do no matter what is being said to you? Do you really believe you can make your dreams come true? I hope so.

I didn't know that when I left my parent's home, that I was Desire strong. I wanted so badly to make it on my own and succeed. I know that there is something in you that you feel so strongly about that you would be willing to leave things behind and go after it, what is that Desire?

The **fourth** thing I want to share, is that you must be Desire Driven. Wow, what do I mean by that it almost sounds like being Desire strong but there is a difference? What I learned about this principle, about being driven, that even in moments of weakness, there is nothing that will stop you from going after your dream. Having the drive to move forward despite the haters in your life, to have the drive despite those who want to sabotage your dreams, the drive to continue even when you don't see a light at the end of the tunnel. That Drive, you see, that Drive will move you from the gate despite the weather conditions, that drive will keep you moving toward your destiny even when you seem like you are in a holding pattern, that drive will make you believe that all things are possible even when others say it is not, that drive will take you from the curb, to the gate , down the tunnel, onto the plane, out to the runway and into the air – That is the drive you want to have for your life, you must be Desire Driven!

Lastly, but not least, one of the lesson that was most important and I hope you see why this played a significant role for me and I hope for you as well. You must be Desire connected. Well John, what do you mean by that? Glad you asked. This is where my foundation comes from, this is what got me through so many storms this is what I believe for you will take you to the other side! To be desire connected, means to be connected to your source no matter what you are going through. Growing up in Church, I knew and understood what my source was and how much I heavily had to lean on it. Now, God is the source of my life and there is no shame in me saying that. You may see something as a different source that sustains you and keeps you going and that's fine, but know and understand you must stay connected to that source as you are being pushed toward you purpose and dreams.

I know my faith in God kept me going when I had nothing else and in order to have the Desires of your heart, remember you must delight yourself in your source – in other words stay constantly connected it, be grateful for it be thankful that it is part of your life and journey. Being connected daily, helped me to get through some really tough times. I know that I had the prayers of my parents over me as I walked out that door to take on the world and every day since, I know that it is for that reason I am here today sharing this story and journey with you.

I hope that the principles that were shared by me in my story will in some way shed a little light, give some guidance awaken some Desire in your heart to move you through the terminal, to the gate, down the tunnel, onto the runway so that you can take flight! It's your time to fly, why because through it all while you are in the clouds enjoying this part of your journey, you can look at all the trials, challenges, obstacles and test and know the You Are A Testimony!

COMFORTABLE...ARE YOU By Justin G. LaRocque

Justin G. LaRocque is a young entrepreneur and a dedicated family man. Being in his twenties, he was concerned for his future and unsure where his career was taking him. Justin found his answers in motivational books and inspirational stories.

In these, he discovered a higher way of thinking which drove him to focus on personal development and self-improvement. This lifestyle change allowed Justin to achieve things he never believed to be possible and became an inspiration himself. Since, he has committed his life to helping others. He proves that providing powerful motivation and inspiration can allow anyone to achieve greatness and do something amazing.

With the willingness to work hard and keep focused, Justin G. LaRocque has discovered that the dream is real and is excited to help you discover that your dream is real too!

www.jglarocque.comwww.facebook.com/jglarocque

Email: justin@jglarocque.com

Instagram:@justinlarocque_

In life, we as human beings go through a lot of difficult challenges and intimidating obstacles all which are looked at in a different light to different people. Mainly, all of these challenges and obstacles have the potential to lead us to the road of fear and doubt. The scary part is that sometimes these fears and doubts can take us into a misleading world of distractions and other misguided paths. Sometime in life we fall victim to the deadly feeling of comfort. Why do I describe the word 'comfort' as deadly? Comfort is easy going. Comfort is feeling satisfied. It is what leads us to good. What's wrong with good you ask? French philosopher Voltaire once said, "Good is the enemy of great." Good will keep you at ease. Good will only get you so far. Good is the brother to average.

It may sound strange at first but as I take you on my journey, you'll start to see exactly what I mean. There are times in life where our biggest obstacles and challenges are ones that we cannot even see. Sometimes we are completely oblivious to these deadly situations. I feel that you have a decent fighting chance when you're able to at least face your challenges. Regardless if it scares you or not, you're still able to size up the problem, figure out its weaknesses and move through it. In my case, it wasn't so obvious, at least not in the beginning.

In 2009, I decided to quit my job as a retail assistant manager to become a full time student at the Institute of Audio Research in Manhattan. I felt like my life wasn't really going anywhere at my current job at the time and I wanted to try something new. I figured that a change in both lifestyle and environment could do me good. Plus, I was in my early twenties at the time; this was the best time of my life to make some changes. I've always had a passion for music so I decided to commit myself to learning all there was to learn about being an audio engineer.

My plan was to be the go-to guy for working with all the greatest artists and bands in the world. I wanted to be able to travel as often as possible and meet all types of big named producers and engineers. And of course, I wanted to make outstanding amounts of money while doing all of this.

As I went through my journey at this school I learned so many different areas of the music industry. Even areas that I was really unaware of, I learned how to use a soldering iron, I learned how to put audio to film, how to properly edit specific instruments on various programs and I also picked up some knowledge on the business side of the music industry. Sometimes in life we open one door and expect another but instead we walk into a room full of doors. The opportunities that were in front of me were quite overwhelming.

I was willing to give my all at each direction. I took advantage of connecting with all of the students and teachers and was sure to give out my business cards. I made sure I was involved in as much as I could. I also used up all of the resources that the school offered. I was sure to study and prepare for every single assignment and test.

Finally, in the summer of 2010, I graduated from the Institute of Audio Research with a 4.0 GPA. I was never an A student in high school so this really made me feel amazing. I truly had that feeling in me that there was no limit to where I would go or what I could do in the music industry. I felt unstoppable. The school helped me build a great resume which included the variety of skills that I learned, as well as my 4.0 GPA, which I was sure to place in bold in a stand out area.

My next step was to begin my research on all of the locations, studios and venues that I wanted to work or intern with. I spent the next week Googling and learning all the various areas in which I thought I'd like the most, although I wasn't being too picky. I made sure to reach out to all sorts of places that needed all different types of audio engineers. Finally, I came up with a list of over 90 different places in which I wanted to send my resume to. I got to work immediately; I did everything from faxing my resume to emailing it. I even passed out physical copies to any place that was open for me to walk in.

After sending my resume out over the course of about three weeks, I sat back and waited for my phone to start ringing off the hook. I knew that it was only a matter of time before people would see my 4.0 GPA and all of my skills and abilities and offer me some sort of job or internship, right? Wrong... Out of the over ninety places that I reached out to I only heard back from three. This resume-to-returned phone call ratio was absolutely impossible, unheard of even! What's worse is that those three phone calls didn't even lead anywhere. It turns out that two of them were looking for a marketing person, and marketing was not something I cared for.

Sitting in a cubicle was not my idea of the music industry. I wanted to be in the studio making hit records or helping set up large concert stages all over the world. I guess I forgot that beggars can't be choosers. I turned down the last phone call out of the three because it didn't look 'legit' enough for me, whatever that meant. I look back now and I could smack myself for thinking this way.

Either way, I was more upset about the idea that I only got three phone calls when I was expecting to get around 20 to 30. I truly thought that my resume alone was going to attract everyone!

Have you ever been in a place where you felt like you were doing everything right, you made all the right moves in all the right places and yet you still fall short? That's exactly how I saw it. I was completely devastated. I was confused and angry. I didn't understand why I only got three lousy phones calls. Did I not write the 4.0 GPA large enough on my resume? Did they not see all of my newly obtained skills and abilities? I pictured a line of people wanting to hire me, not three dead end phone calls. I was furious.

Then I remembered something. It was a saying that I've heard plenty of times from interviews and documentaries and even other students at the Institute of Audio Research. They always say that the music industry is all about who you know, and I didn't know anyone. Unfortunately, I didn't know anyone in the business. I never had that friend of a friend who could get me into a fancy studio and introduce me to important people. I didn't have that family member who could take me to big events and introduce me to any big artists or producers. I didn't have these types of connections. "It's all about who you know," this statement absolutely destroyed me.

After letting a few more weeks go by, while continuing to send my resume out to new places, I slowly ran into the problem of not having any income. I had tons of student loans and other bills knocking at my doors which I was going to have to deal with fast. I needed to get some sort of job and at this point I had no choice as to whether or not it had to do with the music industry. I quickly decided to go back to my old retail job as an assistant manager. I was never happy at this place and never felt like there was any future so I definitely didn't want to stick around for too long. I told myself that I would work here for two to three weeks at most until I could final my true calling working in a studio or at a live concert venue.

I didn't quite get to jump out of this job as quickly as I originally planned. Although I swore that I'd only be at this job for three weeks tops, those weeks turned into months... and those months turned into years! I was stuck at this job for over two and a half years after graduating with my fancy 4.0 GPA. I never realized the danger I was truly in. I use the word 'danger' because as much as I say I became "stuck" I was really more comfortable and didn't realize it. I became comfortable with my weekly responsibilities. Stocking shelves and helping customers with product became second nature to me.

I became comfortable with my schedule and always having Friday nights off (which is hard to get in the industry of retail). I would go out and party with my friends every single Friday. I became comfortable with my weekly paychecks. It wasn't a lot of money but it was enough for me to pay my bills and still afford to go out for a few drinks and hang with my friends. I became comfortable with just getting by in life. But was this it? Is this what my life came down to? Was I going to be here for the rest of my life? I can tell you now; I never had any major future plans or goals ahead. All I did was compromise with myself daily.

I believe a lot of us deal with this in our daily lives. We compromise with ourselves. We begin to tell ourselves how to deal with a situation by just pushing it aside or masking it with some larger irrelevant distraction. We begin to say things like, "I don't like my job but it puts food on the table so I'll do it." "I don't like where I am in life but at least I get some free time once in a while to hang out with my friends." I'm miserable in this career but at least it pays the bills."

I want you to stop and think for a moment. Ask yourself, "Is this it? Is this all I have to offer the world? Is what I am doing right now my absolute calling and purpose in life? I realized that 'just getting by' is not truly living. We are not here just to pay bills. We are not just here to live in misery. I've seen others live in happiness. What makes them any different than me? I breathe the same as they do, do I not? I see the same colors they see; I hear the same backgrounds of life as they do, right? If there are others in the world who are successful and living the life they chose then why can't I?

Well back to my dilemma, my problem was that I fell for the trap of comfort and I wasn't planning on doing anything to get out of it. Mainly because I didn't feel it was necessary that there was anything for me to get out of. How was I going to shake this hypnotic spell of comfort and distraction? I wasn't even continuing my pursuit towards the music industry by this time. Audio engineering was placed way on the back burner. I was too concerned with who had a winning record in the NFL, where the next cool party was going to be or what fun video games were coming out next. Music Industry? What music industry? My mind was occupied on way more important things!

The Dream Is Real

February 16th 2013 is the day I got the wake up call...

I met a guy, about a year younger than me, who was very upbeat, happy and motivating. He had a lot going for himself. He owned a brand new car, a house and even owned his own business. Knowing that I was a year older than him, I thought for sure that there must be some excuse as to how he obtained all these great assets at such a young age. I thought that perhaps he had a rich family and that he was so smart that he had scholarships that paid his way through a great college. It was either this or it meant that I was doing something wrong with my life.

It turns out that he did not come from a wealthy family and he did not obtain scholarships for college. In fact he didn't even go to college and mentioned that he was barely a 'C' student in high school. He also couldn't even afford to go to college if he wanted to. This made me very confused. If none of this was handed to him then that meant that I was doing something wrong.

I was so curious as to how he got to where he was today. How did he manage to run a successful business starting with no real knowledge on how to properly run one? He mentioned that he realized that he was going to have to use the resources that he had in order to move forward and be successful. He decided to start reading books. He read books on business, entrepreneurship, and self-development. He pointed out that just because we're used to learning from a teacher doesn't mean that that is the only way to gain proper knowledge.

He said, "If you want to learn business, I can give you 100 books on business. It's on you to decide to take accurate and consistent action on it." He asked me what type of work I wanted to be successful in. I told him that I wanted to be successful in the music industry. He asked me to name someone successful in the music industry. I said, "Dr. Dre. He's pretty successful. He's a rapper, producer, beat maker, entrepreneur, business man, and he owns his own label and company."

My friend asked, "Alright so if Dr. Dre comes out with a book on how he became successful, you're going to read it right?" I said, "No, probably not" as I laughed and continued, "I can't see how reading his book is going to be beneficial to me."

He said, "Justin, let me put it like this, if you told me right now that you wanted me to drive by myself from here in New Jersey all the way to your house in New York but you didn't give me your address, you didn't give me any type of map, and you didn't give me any directions to your house, I will probably never find your house. But if you do give me your address, if you provide me a map and you give me exact directions on how you get to your house, I guarantee that not only will I make it to your house, I'll probably make it to your house faster than you get to your house! These books illustrate the same idea. They show you a map of how these successful people got to where they are today. These books allow you to learn from their mistakes, failures and setbacks. Don't you think that that's some crucial information that can help you on your journey?"

I was speechless. I never thought of those books like that before. I never realized how much they can actually benefit someone who is going after something similar. This made so much sense to me and really opened up my mind to the idea of trying to read some of these books for myself.

Later my friend asked me one more question that completely changed my life. He said, "Would you rather live your dream or would you rather live someone else's?" I told him I'd rather live my dream, of course. Then he asked what it is that I did for a living at the moment. I told him that I worked at a retail store that I was not very happy with at all. He followed with, "See, right now you're helping someone else live their dream." Those words hit me so hard. I was completely oblivious to the fact that this whole time I've been dealing with work, complaining about the job, doing the work anyway, and here I am not even realizing that I've been building someone else's dream this entire time.

I was completely blown away by this. I was upset with myself, I was angry and disappointed. I knew that something had to be done. For whatever reason, those words that he shared with me that night ignited a fire of passion and determination. I decided that from that point on, I was going to do whatever it took to get myself into the music industry.

The next day, I started reading books on self-development and motivation. I grabbed books by authors like Tony Robbins, Brian Tracy and Napoleon Hill. I started watch motivating YouTube clips of Les Brown and Zig Ziglar. These books introduced me to an entirely new way of thinking. They made me realize that I can have, do or be whatever I want in life.

My discipline became stronger. My work ethic became dominating. I began making sacrifices like not hanging out with friends, partying and watching TV. I realized that I had a dream and that no one was going to hand it to me. I had to take action. I started putting my resume together. It was an out-dated resume since I had graduated back in 2010 and didn't do anything in the audio business in between that time. I was not going to let this stop me however. After putting my resume together I went knocking on doors in Poughkeepsie, NY looking for any type of job or internship that dealt with live concerts and shows. I used to be shy and scared of rejection but I realized that I had to do it anyway.

One main point that I'd like for you to take away from this story is that sometimes you've got to do it...**'afraid'.** There are going to be obstacles and challenges in your life that you may not know how to solve or that you may have never experienced before. You will be scared at times but in order to truly be successful you must face your challenges and do it afraid. Ralph Waldo Emerson once said, "Do the thing you fear and the death of fear is certain." I kept thinking of this quote as I built up the guts to go knocking on doors.

After all of this preparation and hard work, in one week, I landed two internships! All it took was commitment and facing my fears. I was blown away with the result that I got, two internships in only one week. This made me realize that the power of motivation, commitment and having a great work ethic was paramount to success. This was my proof that anything is possible if you just put your mind to it and take the necessary action. I thought to myself, "If I did this in only one week, just imagine what I could accomplish in a month, imagine what I could get don't in an entire year with this type of work ethic!"

I had to keep putting myself to the test. I was so curious to see just how far I could go if I just kept up with reading and studying. Three weeks after the two internships, I was introduced to a man who offered me a paid internship with his audio company. I had never heard of the word "paid" and "internship" in the same sentence so I was very excited. Three months later, I was offered a full time position with this company in the music industry. Ever since then, I've met big names artists and producers and I've traveled all over the world. I've been to Nashville, to California and all the way to Germany even. I never thought that I'd actually be getting paid to go to these places on business. It has been an amazing experience.

Now I'm not trying to brag or impress you when I talk about who I've met or where I've been. I'm trying to impress upon you the idea that you really can have, do, or be whatever it is that you want in life and I am going to leave you with three major keys that can help you get there.

The first key is what I mentioned earlier in the chapter, do it afraid. It's okay to be scared of the unknown but you cannot let that determine who you are and what you do. In order to live your dream you must be willing to recognize the fear and do it anyway. The funny thing is that most of the time those fears are not even real. Zig Ziglar said that fear stands for False Evidence Appearing Real. This means that it's really just something that we imagine in our own mind. I worry about what might not happen, or what might not work, or what might go wrong. You've got to realize that "worrying" is just a misuse of your imagination. So next time you catch yourself building up fear by worrying about something that probably won't even happen anyway, just remind yourself to stop misusing you imagination. Think of all of the things that can work, that can go right, that can happen!

The second key to achieving your dream is that you've got to be willing to put in the work. You've got to be willing to do things that others don't want to do, so that later you can go places that others won't be able to go. Rome wasn't built over night. I took a large amount of hard work and dedication. Your dream will come after you've truly put in enough time, energy and hard work. While others are partying you've got to be practicing. While others are sleeping, you've got to be studying. You may run into long nights and early morning but just know that you've got your future on the line and that if you really want to be successful, then nothing is going to stop you. Hard work beats talent every time.

The third major key to achieve ultimate success is quite clear, leave your comfort zone and never look back at it! As I've mentioned in the before, being comfortable is one of the most dangerous things that can ever happen to you. It tricks you into thinking that life is okay and that one day your dream will just fall into your lap. It does not happen like that. You must be willing to take risks, explore the unknown and take a leap of faith. Your comfort zone will try to trap you into society's way of thinking, to follow the crowd and play it safe. The truth is *feeling safe is unsafe*. Never forget that.

As you move forward in your life and continue to build and create yourself, remember my story. Know that in order to achieve greatness, sometimes you're going to have to do it **afraid**. Be ready to put in the work even if that means that you may be up late and up again really early. Run as far away from you comfort zone as possible. You're the only one that can ever stand in your way and letting comfort get the best of you can ruin your future forever. Stay focused on the task at hand and keep a positive mindset. A 'stand-out' lifestyle requires an outstanding attitude. No matter what you go through just keep moving forward because when you do that, you'll discover that the dream is real and it's waiting on you to make it happen!

YOU HAVE EVERYTHING YOU NEED

Kimberly Schimmel

Bio

Kim Schimmel is a Life Leadership Coach, Purchasing Manager, Speaker, Trainer and Mom. It's through her life experiences and working with coach and mentor, Dr. Ruben West that she has realized her ability to inspire and help others realize their greatness. Through Kim's, *You Have Everything You Need* program, you will discover that all you need is within you, around you and available to you. This will be her first publication to be followed by many to give you the strength and knowledge on how to make it through your darkest days or through a few struggles to reach another level of loving life and being the leader you were meant to be. Kim resides in

Topeka, Kansas with her two young children, Austin and Ainsley.

You can reach Kim on Facebook at FB/kimschimmelinspires or through email at kimschimmelinspires@gmail.com

– Time Lost

"Nothing has transformed my life more than realizing it's a waste of time to evaluate my worthiness by weighing the reaction of the people in the stands." ~ Brene Brown

If I could take all the minutes I wasted worrying about people's reactions to the decisions I made, mistakes and struggles I've been through, it would add up to years wasted. Plus all the time I've spent judging myself. Yes, I admit it, it would add up to years with an S. Thankfully, I have come to realize through transforming my life, that it really is a waste of time to judge yourself or compare your life to another person.

So many times throughout my lifetime I have wasted time waiting for someone's approval or to tell me I was ready to take my dream to another level. Approve of the decisions I made to not go to college, or to not pursue my dream of becoming a professional photographer or silver-smith jewelry maker. Waiting for the nod of approval only left me stuck and finding myself just short of pursuing my dreams because of what family member said or did not say to make me think I would be certain to fail. To play it safe, I'd take a step back from dreaming the big dream and unfortunately, I was left with the memories of people saying, "She had potential"

My Name is Kim Schimmel – Daughter, Mom, Friend, Manager, Speaker, Mentor and Life Leadership Coach. I am busy mom that spends days working as a manager, evenings at dance class or hockey practice, or 4-H meetings, along with all the responsibilities of being a home owner and parent of two busy young children. We are all so busy in our lives and some of us never really take the time to evaluate what's really going on. I finally found out that after years of battling depression, struggling with financial problems, feeling time lost and disconnected, and ultimately my marriage ending in divorce, that I am complete.

I know that sounds strange to say after knowing some of the setbacks I've had throughout my life. But through my self-discovery process, I've come to realize that in spite of my past, I AM COMPLETE.

"When our inner vision opens, our horizons expand." ~ Louise Hay

It wasn't until a friend spoke life into me that I came to realize that it wasn't the things that were happening to me that made my destiny, it was how I reacted to them. I had spent so many years holding onto my past failures, that it was no wonder I couldn't find success. And looking at my life from someone on the outside looking in point of view, one might think I had it all together. I was raising my two children on my own, nice house, nice car and great paying job. I knew there was more to life. I wasn't happy with my personal relationships, my finances, and I worried that I wasn't a good mother to my children. Was I spending enough time with them? I felt bad from leaving them with a babysitter or after school program because I work until 5pm and school got out at 3:30pm. I would rely on the after school program to help my children with homework, I felt bad for not being the one to help. I felt bad because other mothers were able to spend time in the classwork volunteering. I also felt bad for not being able to make the fancy decorated cupcakes like some of the other moms were doing for their children. My son came home one day in the 1st grade and was so excited about a classmate having a birthday party in class and the cupcakes were so cool. He said to me with the most sincere face, "why can't you make yummy cupcakes with ninja turtles on them, like Jacob's mom?" I was crushed.

Not feeling like a good mother was a huge deal to me. I kept on doing what I thought was the right thing and spend as much time volunteering for the PTO and serving on the Hockey Associations Board of Directors. I wanted to be active in all the organization my children were involved. So my life was emails, phones calls and meetings outside of my regular 40 hour work week. My time being able to keep my house clean and free of clutter was becoming less manageable. And it seemed like we brought more into our house than taking out and pretty soon I was overwhelmed by my home. On top of everything else, I was trying to find a relationship and keep going with all the other commitments I had in my life. I wasn't exercising regularly and my weight that I had lost was slowly creeping back on. I was completely out of control in my life. Although, most of my out of control was in my mind and thoughts that surrounded my clutter, I didn't realize what was really going on. I felt like there was no possible way to dig my way out of the clutter, physical or mental clutter had taken over my life.

These are just a few examples of what my life was like before I decluttered it. Before I was able to make the bold statement – **I AM COMPLETE.**

It wasn't until one day I received a phone call from a friend. He called to ask if I had time to go to lunch that day and luckily my schedule was open to be able to meet for lunch. Upon his arrival we began talking about our life and the things that were going on. It felt like we were just catching up because we hadn't seen each other for a few months. And then he asked me the question, hey Kim are you living your best life? And although I had made it through so many struggles and hardships it had left me feeling defeated on the inside even though in reality I had overcome so much I felt incomplete. That question made me think and with my eyes welling up with tears, I struggled to answer honestly by saying, "NO". At that very moment, I told myself that I was no longer going to just survive but I was going to thrive and I'm going to realign myself with vision and purpose. And I started working with my friend, Dr. Ruben West to create my vision of what my life should be so I could live my best life.

By working with a life coach, I was able to activate my potential for success and discover the clutter that was holding me back from being the best version of myself. I don't know if that's how you're feeling today or maybe you have just hit a rough patch in life – but my decision to work with someone made all the difference.

In the next chapter, I will share with you 4 Steps to a Positive Change that I've personally went through and know with the support of a coach or mentor they will help you create the life you want. Uncover the gifts you have and find your purpose so you can truly enjoy life to the fullest.

Regaining Control

#1 Be Open to the Journey

"Bad things do happen; how I respond to them defines my character and quality of my life. I can choose to sit in perpetual sadness, immobilized by the gravity of my loss, or I can choose to rise from the pain and treasure the most precious gift I have – life itself." ~ Walter Anderson

This will be a journey, make no mistake it will be rough sometimes and you will be tested along the way. But the journey to healing and making positive & productive changes has the power to open up the path of self-love and self-empowerment. And it's a gateway to new success. You must be willing to open your mind to be able to embrace the changes that will happen.

- Self-discovery will include finding your purpose and setting a vision plan for your life

- By identifying your vision, you are able to set clear goals

- Clearly see the changes or shifts that are happening which makes your vision a reality

The beautiful part about self-discovery – you begin to realize that all the things people may have said about you, the way you've been treated or the struggles you're endured begin to fade away. As you make changes or shifts you gain distance from your past, it's no longer who you are. You don't forget it or tuck it away – but you are learning the true lesson that was intended and you are able to forgive yourself. Show yourself compassion. And begin to love the person you are becoming.

#2 Reprogram Your Thinking

"As long as you and I allow others to program us in a way that fits their choosing, we are, without a doubt, out of control, captive to the whims of some unknown destiny, not quite recognizing that what hangs in the balance is the fulfillment of our own futures." - Shad Helmstetter in the book, What To Say When You Talk To Yourself.

It's so important to really listen to what we are saying to ourselves. I had to challenge myself in the beginning to really listen when I was feeling upset, sad, or having doubt and worry about a decision, situation or struggle. I would stop for a minute to recognize what my mind was telling me during those times.

Once you understand the impact it can have on your success you will turn to this Step 2 of the process many times as you work through struggles or shifts in your life. Reprogramming your thinking allows you to view things from a different perspective – as I've heard time and again, "you can't see the picture when you are in the frame." This very statement may not make sense at first but once your mindset begins change and you are open to the journey, you will recognize its impact as you realize the lessons you are being taught by the struggles you endure.

For example, looking back at my life I recognize I've always felt compelled to work in the industry where I could help people. I tried working as a medical assistant, worked close to 10 years as a juvenile corrections officer; I've been a trainer at more than one job. I've tried to help friends and other people around me in whatever capacity I could. But not realizing that I needed to help myself and get myself into the right mindset in order to propel myself into genuinely helping other individuals reach their greatness. I had to find my purpose and my greatness in order to be able to help others. And as an expert, someone that can help you reach your goals and show you how to change your mind set to increase happiness in your life I've come to realize that through this process through the process of my own creating my vision and finding my purpose I realize that I can and do help others.

I had this life changing experience through looking at my past with a different mindset, my parents divorced when I was in the 4th grade and it was a difficult time for me because I was feeling so ashamed of what was happening. And one day my mother, my best friend and I were on our way to the store and we happened to see my father walking down the street holding hands with another woman. Being young and not understanding what was the steps and processes a divorce required, I was shocked and confessed by what I was seeing, my father with someone else besides my mother. She stopped the car and in the rearview mirror I saw her argue and take a swing at the woman that was with my father. My mother got back in the car and was very upset and decided to not go to the store but return home. My best friend went back home to her house which was only a few houses away. And a few days later I called my best friend to ask if she wanted to come over, she informed me that she would not be able to come play ever again. Her mother had made the decision that my best friend and I could no longer play together because my parents were going through a divorce. Imagine how upset I was to think that because of the divorce, I've lost my one and only friend – my best friend of all time. And believe me the effect of this memory has haunted me even in my adult life. I reflected this situation as something must be wrong with me. I'm damaged goods, not god enough. I know this may sound extreme to some people but I was and didn't understand what was truly going on. I never remember having a conversation with my mother or father about how this really made me feel but the lasting impression was a strong one. It wasn't until some 30 years later, I was having a conversation with my mentor when we were discussing where the negative, damaging thoughts that continually cause me to hold back or keep me from reaching goals and this story came up. And within in moments of finishing, he asked if he could give me some insight and what he thought really happened. And he begins by saying, if your daughter came home from a friend's house and said, 'Hey Mom, Julie's (made up name) mom and dad were fighting and another lady showed up and Julie's mom slapped her." How would you feel about sending your daughter to their house again? So how do you know that's not the real reason your best friend wasn't allowed to come over any more. It wasn't because of me and what I had done or that I wasn't worthy of the friendship. But it was her mother protecting her daughter from an unhealthy potentially dangerous environment. WOW. I was speechless. After all these years of viewing this as something was wrong with me, I was being completely fooled by my thoughts.

It was Wayne Dyer that said, "If you change the way you look at things, the things you look at change."

- What are some thoughts or memories that are fooling you?

And when you begin reprogramming your thoughts, it will be clearer as to what is preventing you from living your best life. When you are able to clear your thoughts and start eliminating the negative self-talk and self judgment you will see what is truly cluttering your life. It's important to view this as a time to REFLECT TO CORRECT and not a time of judgment or to punish ourselves. Recognizing your worth and discovering new ways to treat yourself and talk to yourself differently greatly increase the positivity you bring into your life. Now this brings us to the next step.

#3 Clear the Clutter

Clearing out the clutter doesn't just mean to reorganize your living space, but you will need to start cleaning out the clutter of negative thinking, people in your life that are draining your energy, and clearing out the clutter in your finances.

"The world hi jacks our passion and directs it towards material things. But nobody gets to the end of their life wishing they bought more junk."

Being able to clear out the excess you are able to clearly see and appreciate what really matters most in your life. Thus creating a peace and calm in your life that will allows you the positive energy to flow make the progress you were searching for in all areas of your life and in most cases moving you to another level of living and enjoying the gift the universe has waiting for you. You feel complete and know you are living your best life!

The most amazing thing I found out through my journey of self-discovery was the impact it had on providing clarity without me forcing it upon myself. When you are open to change and your mindset changes, you can easily recognize what no longer belongs in your life. It becomes so clear. And once I realized what didn't belong, I had to let go of those activities, habits, people and other stuff that was holding me back.

I don't believe I would have made it through this process without having a coach. Someone to hold me accountable for the changes I wanted to make in my life. As you begin to see more clearly, you begin to trust yourself again to dream again, you become more willing to stretch outside your comfort zone just a little more.

For me a big part of the clutter was anger. Yes, a feeling can be clutter too. It's was holding me hostage, I was so upset over failed relationships, unmet goals and dreams, depression and divorce that my anger was blocking any positive energy for flowing into my life. Recognizing that it's present and going through a process of true forgiveness of myself and other, was the key to breaking free from the pain anger was creating in my life.

#Anger Stops the Flow

"Resentment is like drinking poison and then hoping it will kill your enemies." – Nelson Mandela

There's a price you pay for carrying around the angry and hurt feelings – and you use so much energy – energy that would be better served solving every day challenges – being a homeowner is a challenge – being a parent is a challenge and as long as you let someone take away your energy – everyday life challenges become that more overwhelming. You see – it's sometimes we're not dying from what we eat but what's eating us. In the book Positivity – they do a study were they wire people up to a monitor – show them negative images then ask them to look at a screen – ask them to find something on the screen but they aren't able to see it. And the monitor shows they only looked in limited places on the screen – almost as if they had tunnel vision. But the persons that viewed positive images were able to find the answers pretty easily. Anger, Stress and depression can cause true health issues... so that's some examples of the price you pay for carrying around the pain and anger. This is definitely clutter that could be holding you back from truly enjoying life and all it has to offer.

#4 Take Action – Have a Plan

"Don't concern yourself too much with how you're going to achieve your goal—leave that completely to a power greater to yourself. It's not the how that drives you it's the why"

We all from time to time sit and daydream about what we want for our life but how many times do you sit down to write it out and make a plan of action. And you might say, "Ah that's silly to write it down or I just keep it all in my head, I know what I want!" So let me ask you this, think back to the last time you had one of those daydreaming sessions with yourself, are you on the road to achieving the success you had hoped for? Are you in the process of making those dreams come true? Have those dreams that you so wished for already a reality in your life?

Based on my own experience in this area, I am guessing the answer is NO.

The first step to reach your dream is taking action and that includes a very important step, Have a Plan. I had to ask myself if the actions I'm taking today going to get me where I want to go. Are my daily habits going to create the desired outcome? And the only way that you're going to achieve the dream or goal, is to have a plan of action.

There is an athlete anywhere that made the decision to be an Olympic Gold medalist at the last minute. If you really look at the journey for an athlete competing on that level, they have trained for years for the one opportunity to make the USA team just for a chance to compete for a Gold Medal. So when you look at your goal or dream, you have to focus on the outcome and be ready for the opportunities because if you lose sight of what you're working towards or you sit and wait for opportunities, you will not be ready when it arrives. It's disappointing to not be prepared when the moment arrives.

This reminds me of the time my house was broken into and a lot of property was stolen. When the police came to take the statement and gather important information, I wasn't prepared. I didn't have a log of serial numbers of the electronics that were stolen, I wasn't sure how much money was in the coin jar, or the name of the video games that were taken. In the heat of the moment, I wasn't ready and

I couldn't remember most of the stuff I had, and no documentation readily available to hand over to the officer. Since I was unprepared, this made the process of recovering from this setback so much more time consuming and even more frustrating than necessary.

When looking at your goal or dream you have to ask yourself those important questions and be willing to make the necessary changes to open up the pathway to your success.

Write it down.

What do I do with my time from when I wake in the morning until 10 am?

What so I do with my time from 10am until 4pm?

What do I do with my time from 4pm – 10pm?

Now look at your goal or dream, be honest. Am I doing what it's going to take to reach my goal? If you can't find one thing you are doing throughout your day to help you reach your dream or goal, then I suggest you start today, making some changes.

I know from experience that the road of change is difficult and just remember if it was going to be easy then everyone would be doing it. I want to challenge you to invest in yourself and take a trip through self-discovery because

I am confident that you will find that you have everything you need, It's within you, around you and available to you. But you must open your mind and soul to receive it. Be open to the journey, reprogram your thinking, clear the clutter and take action by having a plan and you will find that you have regained control of your life. You will be the leader of your life and live with the peace and serenity you dream of everyday as you face life challenges.

If you'd like more information about my program or you're interested in having me speak to your group, please reach out and connect with me.

Facebook – FB/Kimschimmelinspires

Email: kimschimmelinspires@gmail.com

Phone: 785-249-6508 Follow me on Instagram @ KimSchimmelInspires

MORE OUT OF LIFE

DeMetra Moore

Bio

Demetra Moore, is a certified Professional Development coach, author and CEO of Moore Out of Life, Inc. A graduate of the Institute of Professional Excellence in Coaching, Moore is passionate about helping others excel in both their personal and professional lives. Moore has spread her messages about professional development and career focus to over 200,000 people as a featured speaker for   Live Your Best Life, 72 Hours of Power, Charlotte's For Sisters' Only expo, and other events. The "No More Excuses: You Want Success Go Get It!" author is also a regular columnist for Huami, Wealth Palace and New Growth Hair Magazine. Recently, Demetra was featured at the International Natural Hair Meetup. There she spoke to women about personal branding and natural hair in corporate America.

She began her work with youth groups and children through the Big Brother & Big Sister Program becoming a "Big Sister" which enhanced her gifts of mentorship and peer empowerment. Now she strives to expose young women to new experiences and new opportunities so they will know the world is full of possibilities. Ms. Moore encourages everyone to believe in themselves and to use and enhance their talents to achieve their personal goals.

She provides individual & group sessions, career development workshops nationally as well as throughout Charlotte and the surrounding areas.

Ms. Moore likes to tell others "there are no problems, only opportunities for increasing one's potential on this amazing journey called life." Demetra believes we all have the potential to live life to the fullest. It's not that life is too short; it's that most people take too long to start living.

In July of 2008 I decided to move toward a vision from elementary school, I wanted to be a CEO of my own business. Growing up poor was definitely motivation to not be the norm. I began a babysitting business at the age of 13, and it gave me the love, the sweet taste of entrepreneurship. Once I graduated college I had a plan to become a consultant and build my business. I created a plan to save more started saving money the closer it got to graduation and included all of my graduation money to support me. I knew to implement my plan I had to have funding. After searching for 6 weeks I landed a position in Charlotte, and my life changed forever. It was time to take action and live out my dream.

In 2002 I took the first step to making my dream a reality. I relocated to Charlotte, North Carolina away from everything familiar. This new place was truly unfamiliar and it was stretching my character and professional development. My job paid my bills and afforded me the opportunities that wouldn't otherwise be available to me. During this time I learned that my job was merely a sponsor, a conduit to making my dream a reality. There were times I thought to myself, "There's got to more in store for me." I've worked hard to be in this situation, and sacrificed too much for this to be the big picture of my life. My vision didn't match what I was seeing in my life. " What in the world am I going to do now?" I had to quiet those thoughts as I made my drive back to my studio. "Demetra act now and feel later, get yourself together it's your turn to teach " tonight. You need your efforts and energy to get you through that jump class. So shake it off sister." That was the pep talk I gave myself as I hopped out of the car and headed into the studio. The serene sound of hellos filled the air and my heart begins to smile as I walk to the locker room to change. "I came out and introduced myself and let the fun began.

I love teaching aerobics because it's one of the foundations for how people got more of out their lives. Teaching others to experience life to the fullest was my passion. My work didn't end at 7:30pm when the studio closed. At night I and did the , schedules, and payroll . I was very familiar with the saying that entrepreneurs' light never goes out.

Food for Thought: Be willing to sacrifice for your vision

- What is your vision for your life?

- Why is this vision important you?

- What are you willing to sacrifice for your goals?

I wake up at 6 am in the morning and get ready for day. As I drive to my full time job feeling as if I'm merely following a herd of cattle. The thoughts of turning around and going back home almost consumed me. It's just unfair to feel this miserable, but my job is my dream funding source therefore, I must go get my "sponsorship". My day at work seemed to drag by as stare at the clock thinking of things I could be doing for my business . Then 5:30pm comes, I run to the elevator to get to my car and speed down the interstate heading to the studio because class starts at 6:30pm. I walk in and yet again the serene sound of hellos fill the air, and it warms my heart to walk into my passion. This time, I was manager on duty and enjoying the fruits of my labor. Month end is approaching and it's time to do some billing and evaluate the business goals for the month.

I organize and review delinquent accounts as well as check the deposits bags and cash on hand. This month is looking pretty good so far. As I months pass the studio starts to not perform as well. Sorting bills and the account ledgers depict the true status of the studio. We aren't as stable I as thought, it's time to reevaluate next steps.

When class ends the ladies leave saying how much they've enjoyed the evening and good night. I think to myself this feeling is to rewarding I must find a way to get this business to work on my drive home it's silent in the car. I was brainstorming of ways to get to get traffic into this facility. Regardless of the economy there was value to what the studio provided. Monthly events seemed the best way to generate new traffic. So Girl Nights Out, and parties became our way to show our value in the community. e The clients loved the monthly events and bought their friends to celebrate this new found excitement .

Soon things started to decline again and finances were becoming more and drastic. . The reoccurring membership drafts lessened, and I started to personally make up shortages on bills. I made the basics were in place and ensured my employees were paid, and the facility was still a welcoming place. This situation began to tear at my heart as because day by day my facility falling into the red. My resources were depleted all I had left were was my vision. Life was stressed in all areas during this point. I didn't know what to do or where to turn. I was broke and ashamed because the context of who I was and dreamt about was on the line. It's what I was made to do, and it just not panning out.. My relationship took a turn for the worst and now the very things I deemed to be secure and real **were all in disarray. The vicissitude of my life was taking me to deep dark place.**

Food Thought: Focus on the good things even in chaos

- How do you handle it when your plan doesn't play out?

- When the world is screaming around you, how do you quiet your mind?

- How do you handle the feeling of fear and failing?

I had to decide what my next steps were going to be. It felt as if my sanity was slowly slipping away. . There was no more money the well was dry. My family couldn't help and all my options were exhausted. I kept thinking what I could do to make this work or to change the situation. Could I move out of my home, rent an apartment, or maybe even sell my car and get a cheaper one? I began to think about Steve Harvey and Tyler Perry's stories of hardship on the road to success and wondered how they handled the failures in front of everyone. I went into a low place, and all I had left was my faith, and will to live. So I made one of the hardest decisions in my life which lead to closing the gym and sell what I could. . My studio closed August of 2008, and it felt as though my life was lived under a microscope doors closing bought tears to my eyes, the end had finally come. I knew that it was to close that chapter of my life and t to move on but I didn't know how. I isolated myself from most of my friends and family, because I was in no shape to deal with accepting the fact that I was a failure. Not only did I fail myself, but I failed in front of my family and the entire world. How do I live with that? How do I come back from that? Why did I even make so such a bold step? I'm nothing more than a failure. Were some of the things I said to myself day after day?

I prayed daily to be pulled out of the mental black hole. Then as time moved on I started noticing the positive side of starting the business. I learned how to manage people, build rapport and network on higher level. Those are skills I couldn't get in any classroom, and I learned to face life's obstacles. I began to believe there was a way out of this, but I needed to talk to my network to see what could be done. After I talked to my network the exploration process began. There were actually options on dealing with the debt and saving what I worked so hard for. I started to meet with several attorneys to get legal advice. I began to collect all of the information because I knew I would have to make a decision regarding my next steps.

As the holidays approached it was inevitable that a decision had to be made and not drag this into the New Year. So I sat down with all of the information and began to weigh the pros and cons. This was yet another difficult decision. My heart was so heavy with depression, the failing, bill collectors calling and simply pure embarrassment. How could I have let myself get into this situation was all I could think about. But I got myself together and started focusing on my current situation and what could be done to improve it. The best decision was to move forward with the bankruptcy in hopes to get a chapter 7 to have clean slate. The following day I contacted the attorney and proceeded with next steps. I was angst about meeting with the attorney. My appointment was confirmed, and all was left to do was to show up. When I got to his office he had an enormous case load. It was a relief to know there were others who were having some sort of financial issue.

He explained the process to me and gave me lots of information to complete and he issued an order to have bill collectors stop harassing me. A few days passed and the calls finally stopped, now I could think and not worry about my phone ringing every five minutes with a disgruntled person asking me for money. As I worked thorough the bankruptcy process my focus shifted to great things on the other side of this tumultuous decision. By the beginning of 2009 I was preparing for court to close this chapter of my life. While preparing for court I was able to save money since my struggle to pay bills was over. It felt good to be on the way to financial stability again.

On a cold February date it was time to go to court and finish this process. I was so nervous and a little uncomfortable about going to bankruptcy court. I walked up the steps with my head hung low and hat pulled down just in case a bill collector knew me and came trying to collect on the last day. Nothing could have prepared me for what I saw when I arrived. I walked around the corner and saw the hallway was packed with people waiting for court. When the doors of the court room open we all poured in like kids going to recess. It seemed like we all knew this terrible situation was coming to an end and there was something astounding on the other side of this.

The judge came in and banged his gavel and began to speak. He told the entire room to stand and even those in the hallway who couldn't fit in the room to stand and be sworn in. That moment gave me a huge since of relief. To know I wasn't alone, it was a room full of people with over flow in the hallway that had been through something that led them to this point as well. It's not such a disgrace to be standing here, nor does it make me bad person. Finally they called my name, asked me a couple of questions and he banged the gavel.

At that very second it felt as if 2000 pounds came off my shoulders. I was now free to start my life over....this situation didn't break me. I knew in my gut it was preparing me for what was on the other side of great. I knew the opportunity would present itself for me to start back having more out of my life, and I could use this time for self-discovery and preparation. I learned life is what you make it. There will always be stumbling blocks in your path. However, you build character as your surpass each of them.

Food for thought: You either win or you learn

- How do you handle failure?
- Have you gathered the information necessary to make a sound decision?
- What is your process of gaining focus?

You too deserve more...

About seven months passed and the desire to teach came back stronger than ever. So I contacted the YMCA to see if they had any openings. Luckily people who worked with me previously were still there. They thought highly of work, and offered me a position. This teaching experience felt different. I was able to do something I loved, and walk away at the end of the day. As time went on my numbers grew and people enjoyed working with me.

I was inspired to start challenging my class with goals to push them harder. The word about my "coaching" conversations after class began to spread and people would come by share their progress with me. One day things came crystal clear to me. The very part of the gym I loved so much found its way back into my life again……. coaching and training others. This chapter in my life was becoming quite exciting. This was a clean slate for me, no more debt, guilt, regret, and no more anger.

One day a coworker asked if I was still working with people in the community on goal setting and professional planning. I told her yes and she sent me a link to this school called Institute of Professional Excellence in Coaching. I read about the school, and it seemed pretty interesting so I called to speak to an advisor. The information that advisor shared forever changed for my outlook on life. Who would've thought people get paid to do the very activities I did for free. After speaking to the advisor I enrolled in school to obtain my coaching certification. My new journey was exhilarating and had no idea it where it would lead. I did as Martin Luther

King said, "Faith is taking the first step even when you don't see the whole staircase."

School started that November and I was on the fast track program. During that time I learned Life is nothing but an obstacle course, its all about getting through that obstacle course *successfully* and reaching your desired goal. Nine months later I completed the program, and started what is now "Moore Out of Life".

This situation taught me several life lessons. The most important lesson learned was not to fall into a place of regret. Everything in my life happened for a reason, much like things happen to others. However, those things taught me valuable lessons which I use today while working with my clients.

So, with that said, here are some helpful, tested pointers that will keep your attention focused in achieving any goal that you put your mind to.

Lesson #1: Don't be afraid to stretch your character. I decided to attend school at the New York Campus. I had never been to New York before so this was the opportunity to start a new phase of my life. For you it could be going to school or to a place you have never been. Just take a minute and imagine what it would be like to try something new, or step out to do something you've always wanted. Most times people choose what's familiar instead of what they really want. Fear is the common reason people do that. As of today take control of the fear, and make it work for you. Fear stands for feeling eager and ready, with that being said create your plan of action and get focused.

Understand that it's normal to encounter obstacles in the pursuit of your goal. We are bound to face resistance as we press to grow forward so why not face it for something you really want.

However, when these obstacles start to become a nuisance to the point of almost putting a stop to your goal(s); or worse, making one completely abandon his/her goal, one must take action and think things through.

Lesson#2: Think positive. This means: Do not quit. Especially when one is midway in working for a goal, there should be no room for quitting. To quit is tantamount to going back to the starting line of goal accomplishment. That is time, energy, money, and a whole lot of things wasted and lost. It is more costly to quit than to find a solution to the problem, not to mention the frustration one feels. I understand sometimes it can be hard to be positive. During some of the toughest times it feels as though you win some and you lose some, and nobody wants to be loser. Well I'm telling you as of today there's no such thing. You either win or you learn. Even when things aren't quite going your way, step back take a look it. Then give yourself credit for trying to reach your goal, and review the situation for things you could continue to improve on. Be sure to exhaust every possibility, even to the point of trial and error, just to be sure that there is a solution to correct the problem you're dealing with. This leads to me to Lesson

Lesson#3: Keep a clear, open and tense-free mind. Always be ready to receive new ideas. Focus and concentrate. Think on a wide scale manner and always be open for options (even unconventional ones) to eliminate the particular obstacle you are currently dealing with. You should open your mind to the include possibilities and options so big that it should scare you. Picture yourself with a possible solution to help overcome and/or solve the obstacle that's setting you back. I've heard that if your dream doesn't scare you then it's not big enough. Accept the challenge and go beyond the norm, challenge the status quo.

Lesson#4: Hire a coach. If all fails get assistance from others you know who are more knowledgeable on the work being done. They will be able to help you see things that are not so apparent to you. Your coach can help you discover ideas in finding the right solution to your problem. You will have the extra support system and focus you need to keep your eyes on your overall objective.

Those are the basic 4steps to overcoming any obstacle that's holding you back. Hire a coach who can help provide the structure, accountability and help develop strategies to implement each step. Those actions will counteract the fear of rejection that was fueling some of the fear and stagnation in your life. You'll start to feel more confident and relaxed as you experience the success of reaching your goals. Always remember, you can't control when an opportunity presents itself all you can do is be ready. For more information contact Moore Out of Life at (704) 565-9608 or visit **www.mooreoutoflife.com**

FEAR CAN DESTROY YOU

Dorian A. Branch Sr.

Bio

Born in Topeka, Kansas, Dorian is a Speaker/Trainer with Dr. Ruben West's Black Belt Speakers Organization. He is dedicated to helping youth groups and young adults discover and develop their Full potential.

In 1984 Dorian Joined the United States Navy and worked his way through the ranks to become a Non Commissioned Petty Officer in charge of a small division aboard the USS Kitty Hawk. Dorian continues to serve in the Reserves and has served as the Leading Petty Officer on several deployments and is a veteran of Desert Storm and Iraqi Freedom.

Dorian has served the citizens of Topeka, Kansas for over 26 years as a member of both the Topeka Police Department and the Topeka

Fire Department, where he currently serves as a Fire Safety Inspector.

Raised in a middle class environment by a single mother with the help of a non-resident father and extended family members, Dorian dreamed of doing positive things and helping people succeed and realize their full potential; however it wasn't until he came in contact with his mentor that he realized that he too had a voice and people needed to hear it. Dorian has been featured on the weekly **Radio Show "Peace In Living Today"** hosted by Felice Thompson Pope. Dorian has also been the **featured Key Note Speaker** for the Topeka High and Highland Park High School JROTC programs in which he spoke to the cadets on the power of their voice, letting go of their fear in order to do what is right and what it takes to become a leader.

Dorian graduated in 2005 from Friend's University with a degree in Business Management.

I want to ask you a question and please be honest; has there ever been a time in your life when you have been fearful? If you have ever had this fearful feeling, I want you to know that you are not alone. The feeling of fear is very real and it has to do with both the known and unknown. What is Fear? It has been said that Fear is simply False Evidence Appearing Real.   In   fact,   according   to   the Statisticbrain.com when it comes to fears and worries; 60% of the population fear things that will   never   take   place   and   90%   of   the population fear things that are considered as insignificant issues.

If this is the case, then we need to stop letting fear control so much of our lives? Wherever you are right now, I want you to stand up and say to yourself in a convincing voice "I WILL NOT LET FEAR STOP ME".

It is said that the number one fear is the fear of speaking in public. Now, I don't know if this is true for most people or not, what I do know is that it was true for me.   In fact I can remember wanting to withdraw from my high school acting class simply because I was afraid of getting up on that stage and "looking like a fool" in front of the audience. You see I liked the thought of being someone that I wasn't and acting was a way to do just that, the only problem is you cannot act behind closed doors; you have to get in front of the audience in order to tell the story. Once I realized that no one was going to kill me if I messed up and the world was not going to end; my fear was controlled and I really enjoyed myself on stage.

A LEARNED BEHAVIOR

It has been said that we are not born to Fear. If this is true then Fear is a learned behavior. Take a small child he/she will run, climb and jump from almost anything without the fear of what could go wrong. If they scrape a knee or get a pebble lodged up the nose, it simply is a 'Learning Pit Stop". Fear is most often a result of an environmental learned behavior, a result of our caregivers putting the Negative Cautious Thoughts in our head. I am reminded of the times that I have my 4 year old granddaughter, Maliha and how she loves to go to our neighborhood park to play. Well, on one particular day we were in the park and she said to me "pawpaw, I am a big girl you don't have to hold me on the Monkey Bars". I was reluctant and although I didn't totally walk away and leave her to cross on her own, I did remove my hands and from her waist and just shadowed her as she crossed. After getting off the Monkey Bar she proceeded to run, climb and jump on almost everything in the park without any fear of falling and hurting herself. You see the fear of her falling and hurting herself was within me. If she fell (and she did at times) and she wasn't hurt badly, she would maybe cry a little then get back up brush herself off and keep moving.

How many times have you fell or had a set back and thought that the world was coming to an end? I got news for you and this may come as a surprise but the world did not end so get up, dust yourself off and use your setback as a setup for a comeback. It does not matter if your friends and family say that you are wasting your time. I am telling you not to let their fear of success stop you from pursuing your dreams and goals. Vince Lombardi, the Hall of Fame Football coach puts it like this "It's not whether you get knocked down, it's whether you get back up again that counts".

HOW BAD DO YOU WANT IT

When I was a young high school freshman, I started my high school football career with a bang, in fact I was such a good running back that I started on the Junior Varsity team and saw some playing time with the Varsity team. Needless to say, I as well as all my family and friends thought that I was something special. Now what I hadn't said up until this moment is that I am an Air Force Brat and after living with my mom up until that time, I had decided to go and stay with my dad that year. He was stationed at a base in Northern California, which caused me to attend the local "small" town high school.

This school was made up of the local kids as well as us teenagers from the base. The talent pool although good was not great. After my dad retired that year, we moved to Texas and I decided to move back home to Topeka, Kansas where I could attend Topeka High School and go to school with the kids I grew up with. The summer between my freshman and sophomore years I was working out with some of the guys on the team when one of the coaches came in and asked for all the Backs to come outside and get on the field. Being a running back and a pretty good one who just played in California, I went out to do my thing.

To my surprise when I got on the field; I noticed that everyone was running backwards and doing defensive drills. I asked the coach "where are the running backs"? He looked at me and stated that they are not out here; however you are welcome to stay and join us. I politely said no and informed him that I am a running back to which he simply replied "if you want to play on this team, you will stay with us". What I did not know at the time is that the running backs on this team were bigger, stronger and a lot faster than I had ever been. I had a decision to make. If I wanted to play on this team I had to either get bigger and faster in a hurry or get over my fear of learning something new and change positions.

It might not be football but what is it in your life that has you fearful of change? Is it going back to school in order to complete that degree or is it moving to a new city in order to get that raise complete with the corner office? Whatever it is I want you to ask yourself "How bad do I want it"? It was Winston Churchill who said "there is nothing to fear but fear itself". Stop holding back on your dreams and goals due to fear rather real or perceived.

It is time to stand up to the pressure and face those fears head on. You see a diamond is one of the hardest stones in the world but a diamond does not start off as a diamond. It starts off as simply a rock in the earth and is placed under enormous pressure which causes it to change from a simple rock into that valuable diamond that women adore and a lot of men will spend the their last dime to get in order to make the lady in their life happy.

In life you may have to face tremendous pressure in order to change, but ask yourself "is it worth it"? If the answer is yes, then reach inside you and start the process of making that happen. As my good friend and mentor, Dr. Ruben West often says 'I am not saying that it is going to be easy but what I am saying is that it will be worth it.'

WHAT MUST BE DONE

In my short lifetime of being a single father working three career jobs (police officer, firefighter and U.S. Navy) as well as going to college full time; I quickly realized that in order for me to be successful and not lose my mind, I was going to need help. I had to swallow my pride and ask my family for help and they were more than willing to step in when needed. All that I needed to do was get out of my own way, get over my fear or perceived fear of looking like a failure and ask. Everyone has the ability to resurrect their dreams and get out of the tomb that Fear has put them in, in most cases it all starts with asking for help. Saying I don't know and I need help is a key starting point.

FORGIVE OTHERS:

It is important one realize that holding onto grudges and heartache does nothing to the person or situation that may have wronged you. You see that person whoever they may be has most likely moved on with their life. They are living their dream and doing what they want; all the while you are stuck in the past and can't move forward due to letting past situations paralyze you and steal your dreams.

EXPECT THE UNEXPECTED:

Life is full of if's and buts. How many times have you heard someone say or maybe you said to yourself.

- If only I was born rich...

- If I was educated at that school...

- But I am the wrong race

- But I am from the wrong side of the tracks etc., etc.

STOP with the madness because you have the same 24 hours in the day as the next person, the difference could be as simple as how you choose to spend them. If you find yourself not having enough time, then you may need to get up a little earlier and start your day or stay up a little later. Two extra hours a day is two extra days a month; what would that do for you?

ASSUME GOOD THINGS:

I know that you may have heard this before but there is magic in positive thinking.

In his book "Think and Grow Rich" Napoleon Hill tells us that "There are no limitations to the mind except those we acknowledge, both poverty and riches are the offspring of thought". Therefore it should come as no surprise that if we let garbage into our mind then we will have garbage coming out, and that garbage in most cases will hold you back so let it go. How you may ask? Well, start reading something positive from a good book daily and believe it or not you may have to stop watching the "Negative News" and I suggest that you do. I mean haven't you noticed that the media is filled with a lot of sad stories. It goes without saying that misery loves company.

REACH FOR THE STARS:

In his book You Inc. Burke Hedges tells us that if there are some things that you want out of life, but you're headed down the wrong road, then you have got to change your direction or approach. Jim Rohn puts it like this, "if you want your next five years to be a lot better than your last five years, you have got to make some changes in your life". The changes start with going out and taking a chance in life and not being afraid of the unknown.

In closing I would like to ask you a simple question; can you look in the mirror and honestly say that you are living up to your fullest potential? I want to remind you that this is REAL LIFE and this is serious; there are no dress rehearsals or do overs. This is Showtime and you my friend are on.

If you are tired of letting Fear control your life and are serious about moving yourself to the next level, I would be glad to work with you or your organization. Please reach out to me at:

Dmost45@gmail.net

dbranchsr@msn.com

FB/dorianbranchsr

ONE IN A MILLION

By Josh Rios

Bio

Josh Rios was born in Eldorado, Kansas, but grew up in Maple Grove, Minnesota, where he currently lives. He attended Osseo senior high, where he graduated in 2013, and went to college in Cloquet, Minnesota where he played football as well as pursued a career in sports medicine. While initially pursuing this career in health and fitness he had a change of heart and began working with Dr. Ruben West to become a life coach and public speaker so that he can change the lives of young kids similar to himself and he's been working hard at it for about a year now. In his spare time he likes to read, spend time with his family and friends, along with designing clothes. For any questions and other information email @josh_rios95@aol.com.

In the small world we live in where everyone wants to be somebody and no one wants to be nobody, we seem to forget each one us is one in million, different thoughts, dreams, goals, likes and dislikes as well as stories no two people are the same. My story starts off in 1995 at a hospital in Eldorado, Kansas where I was born to a stranger formally known as my biological mother. I was adopted at birth and blessed to have a family that made sure I at least had what I needed. The reason I even share this part of my life is because it's a substantial part of who I am and another part of my life story that makes me "one in a million".

A look in the mirror

If we are all different what does it mean to fit in? A question I've always asked myself being I never really fit in with anybody when I was kid I was awkward not to mention I was deemed a trouble maker by most of my teachers, and constantly struggled with my dyslexia as well as attention deficit disorder, I had to take special education classes which as you can imagine didn't really help the friend making process and as a result of being sort of an outcast I was very shy and just didn't relate to many others kids.

When you see people constantly distancing themselves from you and you feel judged by everyone you find that you start to question yourself and it slowly begins to kill your confidence as well as our self- image, Maybe you were that kid who didn't have many friends and was the odd one out or maybe you just knew someone like that, regardless we have all been there. The biggest thing that holds us back is our vision of our own selves if we sit here and continuously tell ourselves that it's just too hard, we're not good enough or we just can't do it guess what, we won't!

We all know it's much easier stay in our little comfort bubble then to make ourselves vulnerable but if we don't take steps, how can we possibly progress? We don't! We remain stagnant in that same mental, emotional, and many times even physical state. One thing I wish I had done sooner was step out of my comfort zone, but I'm 19 now and each day I work to make positive steps towards what I want out of life. remember this, **the moment you realize your drive for success means more to you than your fear of failure then and only then can you truly achieve your dreams.**

Your journey begins

I've done it now and so can you regardless of age or your financial situation make a pledge from this day on whether you have to write it down for you to remember or put it in your phone, each day make sure that you make a positive step each day to whatever it may be that you want to achieve and record it you'll be shocked at what you are able to achieve when you decide to move forward and step outside the box, Because as my mentor Ruben West told me "the worst thing that could happen to you is that you'll run into the person you were supposed to be" so what is your next step towards your success story?

Well first we must recognize success is a process a long journey few decide to embark on but since you're reading this I can see that you are committed, so before you decide to travel anywhere you must decide where you even want to go right? So in the space provided write down some goals/dreams you want to work towards achieving.

1. _____
2. _____
3. _____
4. _____
5. _____

Now that you have listed some of the things that you would like to pursue you've taken the first step towards success, you've already done more than a lot of the people who always talk about achieving but never make any forward progress. Now it's time to narrow that list down to a few choices of goals you'd like to achieve whether it's long term as going back to college or simple like just getting back in shape. Along with making goals we also must figure out ways that we can go about achieving cause as we all know success takes baby steps. The next step is to apply yourself, Take what you've written down as goals and figure out ways to achieve.

Bumps in the road

For instance I always wanted to play college football ever since I was young it was my dream and I believed I had what it took, so from a young age I began to progress towards my goal I went to camps to refine my skills, constantly watched football and became a student of the game, as well as working out to be in peak shape, but as we all know not everything goes as planned. No matter how long or hard you've worked, life can change in a split second.

It was the big day of our first game I was excited as ever just sitting at home shaking with anticipation when to everyone's surprise I had a seizure. After that incident I was brought to the doctor and they diagnosed me with epilepsy not only was I scared from what had just ensued but disheartened at the fact I had no idea if I was going to be able to continue to play my last season of high school football.

I told my coaches what happened earlier that day and of course I wasn't able to play but I still came to the game to cheer on my teammates. After a couple more doctor visits I was finally cleared to play I was excited to finally get out there play and have a great finish to my senior year of football but to my dismay that would never happen. After my seizure I never really did go back to playing as much, which hurt because I really wanted to play college football. Being that the rest of the season I rarely got to play I thought those dreams were done and all the hard work I had put in was a waste.

Later that year to my pleasant surprise I received a letter of acceptance to a junior college in Cloquet, Minnesota even after everything that I had been through I was given a chance to pursue my dream of playing college football. It's true that you will most always be rewarded for the work you put in, it may not be instant or in the way you expect you'll have bumps in the road like negative people and situations that will break you down but take my story as living proof that hard work pays off.

Breaking Glass Ceilings

Malcom X said "The future belongs to those who prepare for it now" I have started preparing for my future have you? If you're reading this you are headed in the right direction! If you've been following along you should have a MAP

M: Made a list of possible achievements or goals.

A: Applied yourself to your goals start making forward progress towards your goal and figuring out what you need to reach that goal.

P: Put all that you've learned together and perpetuate success.

Once you've completed each step you've got the map to success. If you can recognize who you are as a person, make it through the trials and tribulations that you will face to get what you want out of life, and break through the glass ceiling that is fear and self-consciousness, really what else can stop you?

I'm Josh Rios and I'm inviting you on a personal journey. Are you ready to break through? After reading through this, chronicle some of your success and milestones you make in the space provided below.

1.
2.
3.
4.
5.

The Influence

Whether its television or the internet, family and even friends, we are fed images and ideas negative and positive so how do we decide what is right and wrong? We live in a world where it's impossible to escape the judgment of the people around us, we now have to know ourselves more than ever. Maybe you aren't society's idea of beautiful, skinny, smart or cool, but forget about it! Do you see beauty and worth in yourself? Because at the end of the day that's all that matters as cliché as it may sound your happiness and positive outlook on yourself is of the foremost importance.

This is why it is so important to understand who you are as a person inside and out. If you know who you are how can anybody else's words can hurt you? They can't! That's the key, to reach a point of supreme self-confidence and happiness that's why I'm here and that's why you're reading this. But I wasn't always happy with myself. In school I spent a lot time in remedial classes with kids who were either slow learners or just deemed by the school to be troubled. I noticed one thing in common between all the kids in these classes with me, we were only told of all the things we couldn't do and what we were bad at throughout the duration of our lives. It starts from a young age, imagine what kind of influence that will have on the behavior of a young kid or teenager.

It wasn't all bad though, there were some teachers who cared and had faith in kids who didn't even have faith in themselves. One in particular has impacted my life dramatically and I'll never forget what she has done for me. Karen Gallagher. She was my math teacher for 2 years in high school and regardless of how I fought her on everything she never gave up on me she tried to get to know me and help me, she helped form me into the man I am today. But it wasn't just me she helped, I've seen her change the lives of many other kids just like me. For that I can't help but be grateful and astonished by the compassion and love she showed day in and day out for people who may not even have appreciated her at the time. It doesn't matter if you're 14, 24, or 64, you will meet someone who will change you. Maybe you can be that someone for somebody out there struggling looking for that push waiting for those kind words to keep them going, think about the **INFLUENCE** you can have in someone's life.

A word, a hug, even a glance can change a person's life forever. Can you remember someone who has changed your life? Whether it was a teacher or a family member maybe even a random person. Whoever it was write down what they did for you and how it's influenced your life to this day.

1.
2.
3.
4.
5.

And now if you have completed this my next challenge for you is to reach out to this influential person in your life and let them know what they have done for you and how they have changed you because who knows maybe you can return the favor and change their life.

Operation Break Through

"Don't think outside the box think like there is no box" we want so much out of our lives but are we really working for it? Is your dream worth losing sleep, friends, and maybe even some family along the way what is your success worth to you? You can ask the best, it never comes easy, For instance Oprah Winfrey one the most influential women of our time had to struggle from a young age to get where she is now. Born in rural farm town in Mississippi with her unmarried parents who eventually split and left her in the hands of her grandmother where she began to flourish, then at 6 years she was sent to live with her mother and half-brothers in a rough part of Milwaukee. Then at 12 to live with her father in Tennessee where she began to speak at church and other social events and realized she had a gift and something she wanted to pursue.

But just as things were looking up she was sent back to Milwaukee with her mother. Things went downhill fast, they didn't have much money and young Winfrey was surrounded by negativity not to mention dealing with repetitive accounts of sexual abuse from men she thought she could trust.

Now if I asked you what are the chances of a young, poor African American woman coming from nothing making it big in show business you would say slim to none right? Even when she was starting to make a name for herself executives shut her down and told her there is no way she could make it on any major network. Now think about it isn't that crazy! Oprah Winfrey, the most watched daytime television host of all time was told she couldn't do it!

Coming from her background she had every excuse to be a loser to just give up and succumb to her environment but she didn't! She broke through that glass ceiling that was her past, she decided nothing was going to stop her from reaching her dreams and she made it, now what's stopping you?

We all have closed doors that we want to open but we have to make a move to open them they won't open themselves whether you have the key or you have to break the door down, all that matters is you achieving your dreams. Nothing can stop you except you. Now is your time, what are you going to do to make sure you reach your goals? We all have a gift and a story. Now ask yourself, are you willing to take the time and put in the effort to make sure everyone hears it. If you are reading this now you've already taken the first step towards *"operation break through"* I've given you the directions to get yourself to that door now are you going to open it or not?

I AM ENOUGH...AND SO ARE YOU!

Traci Ward

Bio

Known as the Women's Empowerment Expert coach Traci Ward hails from Topeka, Kansas. She is a trainer and creator of the life transforming, "I Am ENOUGH" Movement Program. Traci, as a Black Belt Speaker, through the use of her" I Am ENOUGH" strategies continues to carry out her mission of helping women and young girls discover their priorities in life and how to structure their lives around these priorities. Through facilitating corporate workshops, trainings and speaking at events geared toward improving the lives of individuals personally and professionally. She uses accountability, personal goal setting and other methods to help clients realize their fullest potential and to take back or maintain control of their destiny.

She has more than 20years of experience working with youth groups through church and the community. She is a founding member of the group Daddy's Girls, Inc. created by Telisa Haggerty. Ward has gone into community based entities such as high schools Boys and Girls club and other organizations, empowering young girls to be all they can be, to never compromise their integrity and encouraging them to set a "standard of excellence".

Traci has 21 years of service in state government having served as the personal assistant to at least 3 Governor appointed, cabinet level secretaries for the state of Kansas. She currently serves as the Equal Employment Opportunity Officer (EEO) and ADA Coordinator for the Kansas Department of Transportation.

Ms. Ward is committed to helping women navigate through life while discovering their many gifts, and talents. She gives them direction on how to get the most out of life pursuing those things that bring them the most satisfaction. She shares her amazing story of mental transformation and the incredible impact that changing your "mindset" can have on repositioning one for achieving personal greatness.

Traci is the mother of 3 adult children, one of which was chosen as one of the Top 20 under 40 Entrepreneurs of 2013 in Topeka and a graduate of the Class of 2015 Chamber of Commerce Leadership Topeka.

FB/IAmEnoughMovement-tw
Website:www.Iamenoughtw.com
traci.ward40@gmail.com

What would your life be like today, if you knew that nothing in your past matters and has nothing to do with your future? That nothing in your past dictates how your story ends? My discovery of this notion set my life on a different course.

Growing up in the projects of Topeka, Kansas was hard. Surrounded by people who didn't have dreams and if they did, they certainly weren't talking about them. They were simply trying to figure out how to get through the day. . What would they have to do today to see tomorrow?

I've heard it said many times two people can grow up in the same house with the same parents and have two totally different outlooks on life. While my brother and I grew up under the same roof, we took very different paths in how we lived our lives. While I sat and wondered about life most of my younger years, he went out and experienced life. My mom was a single parent, doing the best she could with the tools she was given in life. Later I would learn she hadn't been handed the best set, but she used what she had to the absolute best of her ability.

Having gone through a series of experiences in my younger years I never felt bonded or connected to a parent, so bonding would be a challenge. As I grew up, I discovered there were things that I'd been told at a very young age (by those who had dominion over me) that would begin to shape my self-image and because I believed the lies I'd been told, it set me on a course that wasn't very bright. Being told by an elementary school teacher that "I was not going to amount to anything" was literally programmed into my mind and would take up residence for many years to come. I believed every word she said. At that time she was the most consistent adult figure in my life and had great impact on everything I thought. Her unintentional, crushing opinion, and prophesy was what I believed and was one that played over and over in my subconscious mind.

In his book *Psycho-Cybernetics*, Dr. Maxwell Malts speaks about those things that are present when the subconscious mind is programmed: It's spoken by someone of authority, something that has been said with force and something that's been said over and over. This teacher certainly served as someone of authority and someone I had great trust in. Because of this belief system, there were things I wouldn't even reach for, because I didn't feel I was good enough...

How many times in your life did you not go for that dream job you wanted? Or not pursue that relationship you wanted? Or you didn't start the business you wanted because you didn't feel adequate or felt that you didn't measure up? Often times our dreams have been stepped on by others before we really get to dream.

Looking for Love

My high school years were not the best either. Feeling unloved and unsure about who I was, and having this overwhelming sense of wanting to belong, I began looking for love and acceptance in the wrong places. I quickly confused time spent as being a gesture of love. I believed that if a boy was spending time with me, he must love me and I should give anything I could to keep that "love" present. I lost my virginity at 17 because I thought I'd found "love".

When I realized what I thought was love, left again I couldn't understand why I wasn't good enough. Even though I'd began hearing messages about God's love and how He had a plan for me. I found it very hard to grasp that there was anything "good" that I was deserving of. The inevitable happened. When you don't get the lesson, you repeat the problem.

I repeated it not once more but even a third time. By the age of 25 I had three children by three different fathers and a very bleak image of myself. I decided love didn't know my name and it wasn't looking for me. I concluded, it was just best to pour all the love I had into the most precious gifts I had, which were the most incredible little people one could ask for. I came to the conclusion that love was a one-sided exchange for me. I was capable of loving but not deserving of being loved. I just wasn't good enough... Can you think back to a time in your life when you allowed the things that you'd been told to hold you back from doing something you wanted to do? Or you made the same mistakes repeatedly? Doing the same things, expecting different results, which I've heard someone say is the definition of insanity.

Walking Blindly in my Calling

As the years went by, I remained in a state of pain and confusion. But I was gifted with the ability to connect with children. There were things I'd teach my children and know they were God given, because no one had ever taught me these things and there were times I was in awe of the things He allowed me to pour into them out of my own need...The one thing I knew for certain, was I loved children and I spent time teaching them in any way I could.

I continued to teach a Sunday school class of preschoolers and gave what I was gifted while still living in pain. Later, I joined a group of women doing ministry to young girls in the high school empowering them to search beyond their circumstances. I began sharing with the girls solely because I didn't want them to experience my pain. If I could help one, it would be worth it. Even though I still carried shame, it was the pain that pushed me.

I had been given the opportunity to help girls see that "love" didn't come in the package of a cute boy that spent time with you and told you all the things that made you feel warm and fuzzy inside. That losing yourself in a "feeling" was not what they had to do. When the girls began to show appreciation for my honesty and transparency, this was my first REAL glimpse of worthiness.

Pain Pushed, Then Destiny Pulled

As I continued to pour into the lives of other young girls, and all the while being haunted by "what do they really think of me?" I didn't let it stop me from wanting someone to be better off than I was. I continued to deliver out of not wanting any girl to feel the sting or wear my "scarlet letter".

While scrolling through my Facebook feed one evening, I came across a message that a wonderful childhood friend of mine had posted. He had moved away and experienced many hardships and lessons of his own and now he was spreading this message of "Live Your BEST Life". He had become a coach and this was his mantra.

This message struck me in the most frightening way because these words caused me to think about something I'd never thought about for myself. Others yes, but never myself.

I didn't even know what that meant in terms of my own life and soon the message began to gnaw at me and I found it annoying because I didn't understand the feelings it was causing me to have on the inside and places it was causing my thoughts to travel.

What if there was a life that I was supposed to be living instead of the one I had settled for? How would you answer this question for yourself? This was too much to fathom and why couldn't I shake the feeling of this possibility? Fast-forwarding a bit, my friend reached out to me and we began to talk about his movement and all the great things that were transpiring in his life.

I didn't want to share anything personal because I didn't feel I had anything worth sharing with him and prayed he wouldn't inquire. After a series of exchanges regarding business, our conversation suddenly shifted and with no warning, I found myself confessing that I was not "Living my BEST life".

My friend asked me if I would sign up and commit to coaching with him, assuring me it would be beneficial. I agreed, and as I moved through the process, it literally began to change my life almost immediately. Through my coaching experience I was able to forgive myself for my past mistakes; understand, forgive and mend my relationship with my mom just before she traded this life for one in eternity.

I made the discovery of my self-worth when I discovered my past did not dictate my future. I slowly began to realize and finally proclaim, "I Am Enough". Coaching was my awakening! Through the process I did the hard work and found the balance that I needed. My life changed tremendously. Through my journey I made some amazing discoveries about myself and began to reprogram the way I thought about myself and expanded my thinking of how I see life itself.

The realization that what others thought about me didn't matter, freed me from the bondage of not being able to hold my head high and to walk boldly as I empower others to do the same, in spite of their adversities. I understand now, the things God has given me and how all of my experiences have equipped me to answer my calling and to walk boldly in my destiny of building women and young girls into the strong, spiritual beings He had created us to be. That just because you may have started down a hard road didn't mean you would end up on "skid row"! Prior to going through my life transformation process, it was my pain that pushed me and then suddenly my destiny began pulling me. I no longer speak from a place of pain but a place of purpose.

We often find ourselves in places that keep us from living the full, "all out life" God intended us to lead. Your time is now! When you stop allowing your past to dictate your future, life becomes extraordinary.

Going back to the question I asked you in the beginning. What would your life look like if you knew nothing in your past would dictate what you could be right now? What would you be doing? Are you doing it? If not, what is holding you?

Keys to Unlocking Your Inner Greatness

Through my personal journey and the experience of working with women today, I have created keys to share with you to help you experience life on another level. My clients that I work with, have had great success in changing their lives completely after implementing these simple steps.

Maybe you're the one wondering if you have what it takes to go back to school. Maybe you're wondering if you are capable of having a healthy loving relationship after two failed attempts. Perhaps you're the one sitting on the sidelines of life because the business you dreamed of having was destroyed before you even got it off the ground and you're wondering if you even have the strength or the will to "begin again."

I will share 2 of my many keys that if followed, can give you a new lease on life. If you implement them I guarantee you will begin to see your life change. Not only will you begin to see life in a new light but you will begin to see every aspect of your life differently. New possibilities in what once seemed impossible will suddenly be well within your reach and

166

you'll begin taking the action needed to take your life to the next level.

 BELIEVE YOU CAN

The power of positive thinking is incredible. Once you begin to rid yourself of the negative self-talk going on in you as well as around you, life takes on a whole new quality of living. One of the best places to begin is to:

• Stop Listening to Negative People.

There will always be someone who thinks they know better than you, what's best for you. When you give away your power to make your own decisions you will spend the rest of your life not trusting who you are and your ability to make good sound decisions for yourself. You must believe you have gifts and talents that you were born with. Your critics should never be allowed to sit, "in the front row" of your life.

In one of my favorite books Daring Greatly, Dr. Brene' Brown speaks about the opposite of scarcity is enough. You have to believe that "You Are ENOUGH!" Once I began to believe in myself and think differently about the possibilities of what I could have, my outlook took a turn and began heading in a mind-blowing direction. Suddenly my purpose was clear, I was able to rid myself of negative thinkers and toxic relationships. I began surrounding myself with positive people that were heading in the same direction in which I was wanting to go. And the same rings true for you.

When you discover the powerful being you are and all of the possibilities that are within your reach, that you are able to act in accordance to what you believe and things just open up for you because you have used your faith in the most incredible way that allows you to have limitless possibilities.

You can do and have anything. You have to believe, that not only are you strong enough to build your business again, that God and the universe are going to supply the opportunities you need to be successful in doing so! If you're the one wanting that healthy relationship, the healing process can begin when you understand that "You Are Enough" and that failed relationships do not define your future. In fact they have no place in your future.

They have no bearing on the things that lie ahead for you. It doesn't matter what you've been told by someone else, if you want it, decide you're going to have it. Focus on it. And most importantly. Take ACTION to get it and don't let anyone tell you that you can't have it.

My favorite quote says: ***"Nothing has transformed my life more than realizing, it is a waste of time to evaluate my worthiness by weighing the reactions of the people in the stands."*** Simply put, the

Naysayers in your life should have no voice when it comes to you pursuing your dreams and passions. In the words of one of my favorite quotes Theodore Roosevelt sums it up beautifully:

"It is not the critic who counts; not the man who points out how the strong man stumbles, or where the doer of deeds could have done them better. The credit belongs to the man who is actually in the arena, whose face is marred by dust and sweat and blood; who strives valiantly; who errs, who comes short again and again, because there is no effort without error and shortcoming; but who does actually strive to do the deeds; who knows great enthusiasms, the great devotions; who spends himself in a worthy cause; who at the best knows in the end the triumph of high achievement, and who at the worst, if he fails, at least fails while daring greatly..."

Make the Connections

All we have is now...How will you live the rest of your life? What is it you should be doing that you are not? Do you need help getting there? Make the connection. When we talk about making connections, you may need help getting your relationship on track, so a relationship coach may be the answer. Perhaps it's your finances that have plummeted and you're looking for a way to learn to manage your debt. Or maybe you're looking to rebuild your career and are in need of a career expert. Whomever you need help from, pick up the phone, send an email, or send a text but by all means and any means, make the connection. Invest in your success. Sure, it may not be easy, but the relief that it can supply is absolutely incomparable. Let's face it, change can be difficult but not impossible.

As I stated before, getting a coach and mentor helped me rebuild my life and now, I help women discover their life priorities through personal and group coaching. I conduct trainings on finding your balance in life and how to become a better facilitator for your life. I speak on discovering your greatness and understanding that "Happiness is an inside Job" the greatest love you can have comes from within.

I help women discover who and what is within. I discovered this and so much more for myself. Because I wasn't able to make the changes necessary in my life, on my own and needed someone, with the help of God and a coach, I am now equipped and positioned to provide service to those in need.. I can remember all too well leading a life that had no real clarity of purpose. Today my life is full and my purpose is clear all because one day I made a connection. I now help women break through from the inside out.

What do I mean when I say help women break through from the inside out? Imagine with me what would happen if you took an egg that had a completely developed chick inside. What would happen if you cracked the egg from the outside to free the chick? Yes, it would not survive and would die. But what happens when the chick cracks the shell from the inside and does the work to free herself?

Through the journey and the struggle new life is born...That's exactly what happens with the women I work with. My program is designed to help women tap into their talents, strengths, weaknesses, truths and work from an authentic place of discovery, to bring forth new awareness thus causing them to want to do the work to improve their lives in areas they may not have known were "blind spots" These are the areas we sometimes don't even know they exist until someone brings them to our awareness.

My mentor, Ruben West would often say to me, "Traci, it's hard to see the picture when you're in the frame." Simply put, there are just some things about yourself you will never see until they are brought to your attention. There are practices and habits that we all have that we are unaware of. Have you ever had someone say to you, "You always do (blank) when you (blank) or You always say, (blank) when you (blank)". And your response is, "I never knew I did that!" It's the very same concept.

We all have habits, good ones and some that we would like to change. Through my coaching program, I take women through exercises and create ways that help change the things they want change and strengthen the areas in which they identify, through self-discovery feel they want to improve.   Remember it's not the destination or the achievement of a thing that we get the most fulfillment out of...it's the journey. It's the journey that brings about the testimony!

As I conclude this chapter, perhaps you've found yourself in very similar struggles or something you've read caused you to think about a difficult time in your life or even a challenge you currently have.

Are you in a place of feeling "stuck"? What's holding you? (Lack of motivation, unorganized)

_____

_____

_____

_____

Are you finding it difficult to focus on the things that really matter? Why?

_____

_____

_____

Are you having a hard time finding out what it is that really matters in your life or what it is you should be doing? Write down your thoughts.

_____

_____

_____

If you're having difficulty in any of the areas above they are often coupled with feelings of confusion, disorganization, no clarity, no direction, a lack of motivation the list goes on and on.

I have good news! I can help. As I stated before, I help women identify the priorities in their lives and then we do the work to structure their lives around the priorities they have identified through my coaching program and the techniques I use such as goal setting, prioritizing tasks, etc. When you sign up to work with me, you'll learn to:

- Identify areas of your life in which you want to make adjustments
- Set meaningful goals
- Get organized

- Have more free time to spend with family
- Be more productive with the same 24 hours you've always had.☺

Just as I discovered that I Am Enough. You will discover So Are You

LIFE IS A FIGHT

Robin Shyrell

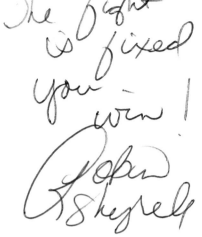

Bio

Robin S. 'Robin Shyrell' Williams is a dynamic, inspiring, transformational speaker, author coach and trainer Her background is as dynamic as she is. She completed her undergraduate studies at Grand Valley State University earning a Bachelor of Science in Health Sciences.

In 2011 Robin ventured in to the 32 Billion Dollar Direct Sales Industry as a consultant with Traci Lynn Fashion Jewelry. She's achieved the rank of Ruby Director as she continues to build a team and assist them with defining and achieving personal and professional business goals.

Robin's mission is to transform the lives of women and youth through her impactful **Moving Forward on Purpose** platform as well as be an advocate and change agent for mental health issues. By sharing her message of hope and overcoming her battle with clinical depression. Her authentic messages are designed to free, empower and restore hope in the place of hopelessness as she assists in moving from a place of existing to thriving. She uses her experiences to help others realize that they to possess the ability to overcome, thrive and win the fight creating the life they desire. Robin is a Christian and proud member of New Jerusalem FGBC. 810-730-8397 rshyrelle@gmail.com

www.tracilynnjewelry.net/rswilliams

How many of us know that life really is a fight? And that we have to take an active role by fighting for what we want? I can tell you for certain that I for one didn't know, realize or understand that life really and truly is a fight. Otherwise I know I would've approached it differently.

Growing up on the north side of Flint, Michigan I was what most people would refer to as a tomboy. Being raised by my mother and her only sister, I grew up in a small 900 square foot house with six kids, myself and my aunt's five children who were more like siblings than cousins. My sister/cousin was the oldest, there were four boys between us and I was the youngest. Fighting was something I was both familiar with and accustomed to. Being small in stature I even had my own philosophy about fighting. I expected to get hit, to take some punches but I was going to be the one to throw the first punch. I was coming out swinging.

What would your life look like if you consciously fought for what you wanted? I can only imagine the difference this would've made in mine if I had applied this philosophy to my life in general. One of my favorite quotes from Les Brown says,

"Your Life is a fight for territory, the moment you stop fighting for what you want,

What you don't want automatically takes over".

Somewhere along the line I picked up that it wasn't lady like to fight and trying to conform to an image I stopped fighting in every sense of the word. I wasn't fighting for myself, my goals, or dreams I was just allowing life to happen. Because life is a fight even though I wasn't fighting for or against life, it was fighting me and I was taking hits and serious blows in the form of life's challenges.

Looking at your own life can you see where life has fought or is fighting against you in the form of challenges? It may be in your relationships, financial or money matters, your job or even grief. Are you fighting for what you want or are you doing what I was doing by just allowing life to happen?

Different is not bad, different is just different.

One of the major life blows life had dealt to me was a sadness that I could just never seem to shake. Even as a child I knew I something about me was different. I didn't understand why I felt certain ways at times, there was no explanation. All I could say is how I felt. And I felt things differently, more intensely than other kids my age. I processed information differently, maybe even worried too much and I possessed a level of compassion for others well beyond my years. The only way I can describe the way I felt back then even now is **blah!** For the most part I dealt with it, a more accurate description would be to say I hid it.

Had I understood that my difference or the thing about me that I saw as different wasn't negative, and that it didn't make me less of a person or a bad person and that there was nothing to be ashamed of - my life would more than likely had taken a different course. I probably would've sought the help sooner. It was my freshman year in college when the difference began to negatively impact my life. After receiving just news from home that one of the more influential father figures in my life had passed away I entered into my first downward spiral. However fear and shame kept me from getting help that I knew I needed even then.

Losing anyone can be very traumatic but this was not my first experience with death. Growing up on the north side of Flint, MI death and I were by no means strangers. By the time I graduated from high school I had experienced death by all means: medical emergencies, natural causes, accidents and even murders of family, friends and classmates. Where I seemed to always recover in the past the darkness that accompanied the death of my father figure seemed to have taken up permanent residence. I remember days of not leaving my dorm room, the moodiness, and the crying.

Is there an area of your life in which you know you need help but fear, shame embarrassment or even not knowing where to turn is keeping you from seeking assistance?

If you don't deal with your emotions your emotions will deal with you..

Inspite of the darkness and feelings of blah I limped through college and even managed to graduate. I desperately tried to avoid situations that caused me emotional drain. But life is life, andlife is a fight; life kept happening and I kept getting punched. My method of dealing with things was to simply ignore them, so I buried my emotions and the darkness kept growing.

I got what I considered a good break when I was hired as first line supervisor for one of the big three American automakers. No it wasn't the job of my dream but the salary was good and there was opportunity for advancement. I made work my everything. It became my way of not dealing with life. Disappointment after disappointment, one failed relationship after another, and death after death, with each punch life handed me instead of allowing myself to feel, to heal or to grow I buried myself in my job. I became the super employee. This allowed me to excel professionally even though personally I was a wreck. The only problem is I wasn't living I was merely existing. Internalizing all my problems and not dealing with my emotions was taking a toll on my mental, emotional and physical well-being. The darkness continued to grow until it started to spill over into every other area of my life. Twenty years later, having received no consistent or effective help I decided that I was tired. I was tired being knocked down in the fight of life. I was tired of smiling all day at work and then crying until I fell asleep. I was mentally, emotionally & physically exhausted tired of trying to be okay so that everyone would be comfortable. Something had to change.

How did I get here?

Have you ever had an experience in your life that made you stop and ask yourself How did I get here? You had goals, dreams and desires but life somehow sent you on a different path and all you can think is how did I get here? My moment came in July of 2009 weeks before my 20th High School Class Reunion.

Standing at the nurses station of 7 Central I asked the nurse if I could please keep my Chap Stick, "It's against policy" she replied, "but I can call down to the pharmacy and have them send up some petroleum jelly for you".

"Could you please" I replied *"Thank-you"* I said as I humbly walked back to my room.

I looked around my bare hospital room, looked at the piece of stainless steel replacing a glass mirror in the bathroom, looked at my gym shoes sitting there next to my bed missing there laces and thought to myself how did I get here? How did I get to the point that at 38 years old here I am asking for permission to have Chapstick, my Chapstick, this is not how my life is supposed to be...all I could think was How did I get here?

Now you may be wondering what about asking for Chapstick is a how did I get here moment. Well 7 Central is a special floor of the hospital, its located away from the rest of the patient wings. It requires you to use a special set of elevators to access this floor, but the most significant thing about 7C is that you can check yourself in but you need a doctors permission to leave. Leaving against medical advice is not an option here because you can be forced to stay by a court order. 7-Central is the psychiatric ward of the hospital where I had been admitted after a failed suicide attempt.

Nothing in my childhood including being abandoned by my father or being raised by a single mom in Flint, MI would have ever lead me to believe that I would get to the point of wanting to end my life.

A Sigh of Relief

"What's wrong with me? Why can't I get it together? Why do i feel this way?" I asked myself these questions repeatedly. Negative thoughts ran through my mind like a song on repeat. By most others standards I had a good life, I had just spent a week in New Orleans at the Essence Festival with my girls and the following week in Negril Jamaica with my best friend for my sister's wedding. But there was a battle going on inside of me, one that I'd been fighting alone with everything in me for more than fifteen years. And now after all this time this battle, unbeknown to even my closest friends and family was getting the best of me and I was physically, emotionally and mentally tired.

Sitting in church that Sunday I pleaded with God, *"there has to more to life than this. God please show me a sign. Do something to let me know I'm still supposed to be here. I'm just tired. If this is all there is to it then I don't want it anymore. I'm just tired. "* As an avid music lover, praise and worship usually breaks down any barriers. But that day I felt nothing. When people asked how I was doing, I mechanically replied fine. No one saw the level of despair in my eyes. As I drove home I actually felt relieved. I had made a decision. "Today would be the end of my suffering, this is going to be the last day of my life" I said to myself.

I pulled my car into the garage went into my apartment poured a drink and began to text my goodbyes. I've heard that a person who "really" wants to commit suicide just does it but if your whole life has been one of making sure others around you are okay which is what my life had been as much as I wanted to be free I was still thinking of the people I loved and I didn't want any of them to feel like they should have done something. I wanted them to know that it was no one's fault, that I was really just tired.

With my drink in hand I walked back to my garage got in my car and closed the garage door. Fred Hammond's CD was playing, I was texting and drinking. My final message said "I'm tired of talking. Just remember that I love you, think happy thoughts of me and not about today." I turned my phone off, took another drink and closed my eyes. I don't know how long I was in the garage before they found me. Everything seemed to be moving in slow motion as the door raised and I was pulled from the car. The rest of that day is sketchy the thing next I remember clearly is the intake process in the emergency room. Little did I know I was about to crash head first into the mental health system. What had up to now been my very private battle was now about to become a very public war.

After meeting with the doctor I now had a name for this feeling that caused me to cry when nothing was "wrong" and I had a name for the darkness, I was diagnosed with major clinical depression.

You don't have to stay there!

If you like me have found that life has taken you to place you didn't desire to be and you've found yourself asking how did you get here, or you just know that you want more out of life I have some great news. You don't have to stay there! You may be struggling with depression, financial challenges, failed relationships, employment issues or even low self-esteem whatever the challenge is, you don't have to stay in that position. I've learned and accepted the fact the depression doesn't define me nor do the challenges or punches life has thrown at you define you. Isn't it wonderful to know that our mis-steps, bad decisions and even our failures do not define us or our future? One of my favorite quotes sums it up by saying:

"I am not what happened to me, I am who I chose to become"- Carl Jung

In the next chapter I'm going to share with you a couple of my F.I.G.H.T principles that have helped me and others fight to create the life we desire. These tips and strategies if implemented will help you regain control in your life. They are designed to transform lives from a place of existing to one of thriving.

They will change your life as you begin to **Move Forward on Purpose**.

After the suicide attempt, I began to receive treatment for the depression. I saw counselor after counselor, Psychiatrist after Psychiatrist and took medication after medication but these things only made the depression, the darkness bearable. I was still merely existing and I still found it hard to believe that this was all there was to life. I wanted more, I needed more. And if I was going to survive this depression I had to have more. I just wasn't sure how to get there.

Moving Forward on Purpose

"My Mission in life is not merely to survive but to thrive, and to do so with some passion, some compassion, some humor and style." –Dr.Maya Angelou

A couple of years had passed since the initial attempt and although I was experiencing slightly better living through chemistry by taking my medication I was far from thriving. I wanted more, I needed more from life. In spite of my mental health challenge I continued to be successful at work but I was still struggling to put the pieces back together in my personal life. In 2011 my sister introduced me to a business opportunity in the field of direct sales. My immediate response was probably the same as most others "I am not a sales person".

There is no growth in your comfort zone.

I spoke with my sister almost daily and she always seemed to be so excited about her new business ventures in direct sales. Although I was far from debt free I didn't feel like I needed anything to supplement my income. Well just listen to the business opportunities she urged. I agreed to do so. The first business I knew I had absolutely no interest in, but on the opportunity call for the second business I heard something a little different.

Still convinced that I was not a salesperson I supported my sister by having a show and even purchasing some of the beautiful jewelry but I didn't think it was for me. I wasn't comfortable with sales. After more prompting by my sister I eventually joined the Traci Lynn Fashion Jewelry business not even fully understanding what that meant. The initial reason for signing up was to have something in common with my sister. I had no idea the impact that single decision would have in changing my life. While work was still my personal and professional outlet I was now a part of something much bigger than myself and seeds were being planted in my mind. I eventually began to participate in the motivational calls and my mind was being expanded. I was slowly stepping outside of my comfort zone and I was growing.

As I worked to change my life I was involved in counseling four days a week. During one of my many counseling sessions with my pastor he asked the question, *"You always seem to have music playing what are you listening to? And what do you watch on TV?"* I had not given a lot of consideration to either. I've already told you of my love for music well during the dark days when I couldn't or wouldn't leave the house the TV had become my new best friend. This brings me to my first point.

-Guard your gates

Our eyes and our ears are two of our senses that allow us to interact and experience the world around us but they also function as gateways to our hearts and minds. The word of God instructs us in various verses to guard both. What we see with our eyes and hear with our ears feeds our spirit. So think for a minute about not only the content of what you watch or listen to but also think about how much time was spent. One of my coaches James Johnson once told me that time is one of our most precious resources because we can never get it back. What are you feeding your spirit?

In the space below identify what types of music and audio programs you've listened to in the past 48 hours:

_____

_____

_____

Was the music or audio programs positive, uplifting, and edifying in nature

or have they helped you to develop a new or improve upon a skill?

_____
_____
_____

Can you identify a better use of this time?_____ If so list what you could've done with it below:

_____
_____
_____

     Many times in life when we face hardships or challenges we may find ourselves asking "Why Me?" or „"Why my family?" and although it may seem some people have an easier life or a life filled with less challenges one thing you can be sure of is that every person experiences some type of challenge. But what if for a moment we change our perspective concerning our challenges. Two of my favorite scriptures from the bible are:

My brethren, count it all joy when you fall into various trials, knowing that the testing of your faith produces patience. James 1:2-3 NKJV and

And we know that all things work together for good to those who love God, to those who are the called according to His purpose. Romans 8:28 NKJV

So by putting my challenge with depression in context with these two scriptures the question was changed from why me to what's the purpose behind it? On a training call with Dr. Ruben M. West he once stated, ***"Apple trees don't eat apples, the fruit it bears is for someone else."*** Hearing those words I immediately thought my fruit is for someone else. The fruit of experience which you have could be exactly what someone else needs this brings me to my next point:

-Help someone else

What punches or challenges has life dealt you that have you trying to identify its purpose in your life?

_____

_____

_____

How can you use your experience or challenge to help someone else?

_____

_____

_____

If you don't see how you can use your challenge to help someone else simply list five ways or things you can do to brighten someone's day or be a blessing in their life.

1.

2.

3.

4.

5.

Now take time today to complete the five things on your list. In the space below document how helping someone else made you feel:

Earlier in the chapter I mentioned going to counseling, seeing a psychiatrist and working with a coach these all bring me to the final point I'm going to share:

-Invest positively in you

Everything that we're doing today is an investment into our tomorrow. So its not a question of whether or not you will invest in you, the real question is are you making a wise investment? It is a positive investment? Will it yield a positive return? I'm sure you've heard the phrase "Success leaves clues" what success clues are you following? Do you have a coach or mentor in the area in which you desire to improve? Think about this if you already knew how to do it on your own you would already be doing it. Coaches and mentors provide valuable insight, direction and guidance. It was one of my coaches that made me realize that the medicine was only designed to stabilize me so that I could create the type of life I desired. It was also through a coaching session that I discovered a possible cause of my physical exhaustion was due to sleep apnea. Coaches and mentors are essential to achieving next level performance or living.

What area(s) of your life would you like a coach to help you achieve next level success?

_____

_____

_____

Do you know a coach that specializes in that area? _____ If not would you like assistance to find a coach?

_____

_____

_____

I've shared with you three points to help you succeed in the fight of life. I am an overcoming expert gifted in dealing with life's challenges. I am committed to helping women and young people win the fight of life by creating the type of life one desires.

Life is an opportunity, benefit from it.
Life is beauty, admire it.
Life is a dream, realize it.
Life is a challenge, meet it.
Life is a duty, complete it.
Life is a promise, fulfill it.
Life is sorrow, overcome it.
Life is a song, sing it.
Life is a struggle, accept it.
Life is an adventure dare it.

Life is luck, make it.
Life is too precious, do not destroy it.
Life is life, fight for it.
–Mother Teresa

If you or someone you know needs to get back in the fight now is the time to take action. Make a decision to **Move Forward on Purpose**! I'm looking forward to working with you on this journey.
Life is a fight, but I want you to know the fight is fixed and YOU WIN!

Robin Shyrell
robinshyrell@gmail.com
810-730-8397

Dr. Ruben West

Born in Topeka, Kansas, Ruben is known as The Vision Breakthrough Expert. He is the founder of "The Success Immune System", a Professional Certified Success Coach, trainer, entrepreneur, published author, and dynamic speaker. He teaches and trains students and clients all over the world to step into their vision and achieve their personal greatness.

Ruben is a decorated combat veteran who proudly served with the 410th Evacuation Hospital as a Non-Commissioned Officer in Charge (NCOIC) during Operation Desert Shield/Storm in Saudi Arabia.

Ruben co-founded several businesses including The Elite School of Surgical First Assisting, a surgical assistant training program, Professional Martial Arts in Topeka, Kansas which recently celebrated its 16th anniversary. Ruben is currently a 7th degree black belt and was inducted into the US Martial Arts Hall of Fame as "Instructor of the Year" in 2005.

After starting several business generating millions of dollars, Ruben developed a masterful coaching system that allows individuals to increase productivity, improve relationships and spend time doing what matters most. Ruben's mantra is, "Live Your BEST Life".

Ruben currently lives in Central Illinois with his wife, Robin. He has a daughter, Monica, and two sons, Spencer and Robinson

25943870R00111

Made in the USA
San Bernardino, CA
15 November 2015